SERVICE LEARNING:

Curricular Applications in Nursing

SERVICE LEARNING
Curricular Applications in Nursing

Gail P. Poirrier
RN, DNS

JONES AND BARTLETT PUBLISHERS
Sudbury, Massachusetts
BOSTON   TORONTO   LONDON   SINGAPORE

National League for Nursing

World Headquarters
Jones and Bartlett Publishers
40 Tall Pine Drive
Sudbury, MA 01776
978-443-5000
www.jbpub.com
info@jbpub.com

Jones and Bartlett Publishers Canada
2406 Nikanna Road
Mississauga, ON L5C 2W6
CANADA

Jones and Bartlett Publishers International
Barb House, Barb Mews
London W6 7PA
UK

Library of Congress Cataloging-in-Publication Data

Poirrier, Gail P.
     Service learning : curricular applications in nursing / Gail P. Poirrier.
     p. cm.
     Includes bibliographical references and index.
     ISBN 0-7637-1429-1
     1. Nursing—Study and teaching. 2. Student service. 3. Community health nursing.
     I. Title

     RT73 .P64 2001
     610.73'071—dc21   00-055581

Production Credits
Acquisitions Editor: John Danielowich
Production Editor: AnnMarie Lemoine
Editorial/Production Assistant: Christine Tridente
Director of Manufacturing and Inventory Control: Therese Bräuer
Cover Design: AnnMarie Lemoine
Design and Composition: Carlisle Communications, Ltd.
Printing and Binding: Malloy Lithographing
Cover Photographs Courtesy of Gail P. Poirrier

Printed in the United States of America
03 02 01 00   10 9 8 7 6 5 4 3 2 1

Preface

Service learning coupled with community-based nursing education is a definitive strategy that will assist educators to prepare nurses for the 21st century. Health professional programs and schools must assume a more active leadership role in preparing tomorrow's practitioners and in shaping the direction of our nation's health care system. To do this, nursing education has to expand future nurses' abilities and clinical competencies to meet society's evolving health care needs. Teaching/learning methodologies need community integration, beyond the current experiential mode. As educators and professionals, our primary purpose is to educate those who will follow us in the future for the betterment of society. This book serves as a guide as we consider our purpose.

My special thanks go to Dr. Charles Palmer, Dean of Community Service at the University of Louisiana at Lafayette, and the university administration for orchestrating the learning environment for service learning to flourish. Through your efforts, you sparked innovation among the nursing faculty.

I am most grateful to the Department of Nursing faculty members who have accepted the directive to develop and implement service learning within their own courses. Thank you for your unfailing creativity and risk taking and for striving to be futuristic.

To my family, I love you and thank you for your endless support and caring.

To the readers of this book, please share your thoughts about service learning with me. With pleasure, I offer my assistance in guiding you with your service learning projects. Write your comments and questions to Dr. Gail P. Poirrier, Acting Dean and Professor of Nursing, University of Louisiana at Lafayette, P.O. Box 42490, Lafayette, LA 70504, or e-mail to *jdc6124@louisiana.edu.*

Dr. Gail P. Poirrier

INTRODUCTION

What do students learn about service to humankind? How do students learn service concepts? Can students apply theory to the community at large? Can they make a difference? What should students learn? These are some of the basic questions that faculty address when teaching/learning outcomes are evaluated in terms of preparing future nurses to be equipped to function in a primary health care practice environment.

Approximately three years ago, the University of Louisiana at Lafayette (formerly the University of Southwestern Louisiana) adopted service learning, created a university-wide service learning council, and appointed a service learning dean. Nursing immediately began the task of incorporating service learning into its practice-oriented curriculum. This task has been a steady process involving students, faculty, and community partners. Service learning objectives and activities have been developed across the nursing curriculum at the University of Louisiana at Lafayette in a baccalaureate nursing program of studies consisting of approximately 650 nursing majors enrolled in clinical nursing courses. Faculty are engaged in applied and instructional research related to the implementation of such curricular strategies. The positive results of this curricular undertaking provide the impetus for this book.

Over the last two years, there have been many professional journal articles and nursing conferences/workshops relative to service learning and its meaning and importance to nursing education and practice. Service learning, as a means for academicians to better connect with the current primary health care focus, community, and expansion of nursing research, has prompted widespread attention. Audiences seem to want more information about the definition and concepts of service learning and details as to how to incorporate and implement service learning in their curricula. Thus, the purposes of this book are:

- to inform educators as to the importance of service learning to nursing education, practice, and research;
- to explain service learning concepts within the context of community-based nursing;

- to give details of how to incorporate service learning activities into professional nursing curricula; and
- to present effective service learning and community-based education activities currently employed in nursing curricula.

This book emphasizes service learning and community-based education across the nursing curriculum at the University of Louisiana at Lafayette. As a result, the book's primary audience includes faculty members in nursing education and associated health disciplines; however, all content in this book is applicable to other disciplines. As a whole, it seems that college educators need a book to guide them in incorporating and implementing service learning concepts within their curriculum.

At the start, this book provides an introduction to the principles and concepts of service learning. The impact of service learning on nursing education, practice, and research when employed in community-based settings is presented. Service learning is linked with community-based nursing education and is presented as a powerful teaching/learning strategy that helps students learn while helping communities to help themselves. Service learning is viewed as a mutually reciprocal partnership that bridges the gap between professional education and society. Actual examples of effective service learning and community-based strategies being utilized at the University of Louisiana at Lafayette and across the country in professional nursing programs of study are presented in detail.

Dr. Gail P. Poirrier

ACKNOWLEDGEMENTS

EDITOR

Gail P. Poirrier, DNS, RN
Acting Dean and Professor
College of Nursing and Allied Health Professions
University of Louisiana at Lafayette
Lafayette, LA

CONTRIBUTING AUTHORS

Anne Broussard, DNS, CNM, FACCE
Associate Professor
College of Nursing and Allied Health Professions
University of Louisiana at Lafayette
Lafayette, LA

Lisa Broussard, RNC, MN
Instructor
College of Nursing and Allied Health Professions
University of Louisiana at Lafayette
Lafayette, LA

Nancy Debasio, PhD, RN
President and Dean
Research College of Nursing
Kansas City, MO

Carolyn Delahoussaye, DNS, RN
Associate Professor and Coordinator,
Master of Science in Nursing Program
College of Nursing and Allied Health Professions
University of Louisiana at Lafayette
Lafayette, LA

Jill Laroussini, RN, MSN
Instructor
College of Nursing and Allied Health Professions
University of Louisiana at Lafayette
Lafayette, LA

Sara C. Majors, PhD, CRNP
Assistant Clinical Instructor
Infant/Neonatal Nurse Practitioner
Program
College of Nursing
University of South Alabama
Mobile, AL

Gary Marotta, PhD
Former Vice President for Academic Affairs
University of Louisiana at Lafayette
Provost and Vice President for
Academic Affairs
State University of New York College
at Buffalo
Buffalo, NY

Pamela Martin, MSPT, MPH
Assistant Professor
Department of Physical Therapy
University of South Alabama
Mobile, AL

John P. McGuinnes, MD
Medical Director
Clinica del Megrante
Alabama Department of Public Health
Baldwin County
Mobile, AL

Mary B. Neiheisel, EdD, RN
Professor
College of Nursing and Allied Health
Professions
University of Louisiana at Lafayette
Lafayette, LA

Charles E. Palmer, PhD, CCS
Dean, Community Service and Head
Department of Sociology and
Anthropology
University of Louisiana at Lafayette,
Lafayette, LA

Sandra J. Peterson, PhD, RN
Professor and Department Chair
Nursing Department

Bethel College of Nursing
St. Paul, MN

Belinda Poor, RN, MSN
Instructor and Coordinator
Continuing Education Nursing Program
College of Nursing and Allied Health
Professions
University of Louisiana at Lafayette
Lafayette, LA

Susan W. Reynolds, RNC, MS
Instructor
College of Nursing and Allied Health
Professions
University of Louisiana at Lafayette
Lafayette, LA

E. Joe Savoie, EdD, MEd
Commissioner of Higher Education
State of Louisiana
Baton Rouge, LA

Marjorie A. Schaffer, PhD, RN
Professor
Nursing Department
Bethel College
St. Paul, MN

Helen Sloan, DNS, RN, CS
Assistant Professor
College of Nursing and Allied Health
Professions
University of Louisiana at Lafayette
Lafayette, LA

Carolyn White, RN, MSN
Assistant Professor
College of Nursing
University of South Alabama
Mobile, AL

Jerry L. White, PhD, RN
Assistant Professor
College of Nursing and Allied Health
Professions
University of Louisiana at Lafayette
Lafayette, LA

CONTENTS

CHAPTER

SERVICE LEARNING AND COMMUNITY-BASED NURSING: A NATURAL PARTNERSHIP

Dr. Gail P. Poirrier

Partnerships between community-based entities and academicians are receiving more recognition as a means of evolving evidence-based practice and policy directions in health care delivery systems (McWilliam, Desai, & Greig, 1997). In this era of partnerships, there is a rising increase in collaborative relationships between the academic professionals and varied professional and lay entities, from individuals and families to whole communities and business, civic, government, and religious organizations (U.S. Department of Health and Human Services, 2000). Such partnerships are reciprocal in that both entities meet their own needs for future growth and development.

Since the 1800s, nursing education has traditionally embraced community and public health concepts of care as a means to promote health and to prevent illness. Florence Nightingale's work in the Crimean War in 1853 followed by the establishment of a nursing training program set the stage for nurses to develop relationships with the poor and underserved families in the home setting and for involvement in government legislation to ensure public health (Cookfair, 1996).

Over the years, advancements in science, medicine, and technology reshaped health care systems. Prior to the early 1990s, our country focused on illness and sophisticated, highly specialized treatment of individual health care needs, not population-based or public health services (Shoultz & Amundson, 1998). Nursing practice was hospital-based, and nursing education prepared nurses to work in acute care and tertiary care institutions. As a result of national and global health care initiatives, such as Healthy America Practitioners for 2005 (Shugars, O'Neil, & Bader, 1991), the World Health Organization (1978), the World Health Organization Study Group (1986), and *Community Partnerships: An Initiative in Health Professionals' Education* (Richards, Grace, & Henry, 1991), the focus of health care systems shifted to its current focus on primary health care. An agenda for action plan noted that primary health care practitioners for 2005 should expand their abilities and clinical competencies specifically to some of the following areas to meet society's evolving health care needs (Shugars, O'Neil, & Bader, 1991):

- community collaboration and participation
- diversity and multiculturalism
- cost effective and appropriate health promotion
- disease prevention
- accessibility
- coordination and management of primary care
- interdisciplinary collaboration

The agenda for action plan (Shugars, O'Neil, & Bader, 1991) also recommended that health professional schools provide leadership in the preparation of future practitioners and in shaping the values and direction of the entire health care system. Nursing education responded by increasing student learning experiences that took place in a community context.

Nursing education must fast-track professional nursing curricula to better reflect the transition from illness to health and wellness in the preparation of future nurses. This is a difficult and challenging task for nursing education. Nursing education cannot discard all that is valuable within its discipline and own unit or department within its institution. For example, the highly sophisticated, technology trained, and specialty educated nurse who can give specialized care in acute and tertiary care settings is much in demand and is necessary for the health of our nation. However, the challenging task at hand is the inclusion of the new skills and knowledge base in nursing curricula that are necessary to prepare nurses to apply their education and skills in community-based settings. In creating new models for curriculum development, nursing education must find new models that permit new ways of organizing knowledge, faculty, research, and clinical learning experiences for patient care (Shugars, O'Neil, & Bader, 1991). In essence, nursing education curricula need to be purposefully restructured into active learning programs of study. Service learning, an active learning strategy, can create new pathways for successful and immediate curricular change.

By virtue of the nature of nursing education, nursing faculty and students have connected with various aspects of the community within the definition of public health and community health nursing practice. Nursing education has a history of interfacing with health care professionals and individuals and families in varied settings within the community, particularly in clients' homes and public health or community clinics. With the incorporation of service learning concepts and innovative curricular strategies, nursing education can now venture beyond the traditional norms of the typical experiential and community learning settings. This new direction in service guides nursing faculty and students to "do with" rather than "do for" (Henry, 1999). Nursing education must interface with all aspects of the community and must develop community partnerships for the good of the students, faculty, the educational institution, and the community at large.

Service learning can assist nursing education to develop and create their own autonomous learning environments and community-based partnerships. Community-based partnerships built on the principles of service learning provide for collaboration and sharing of common interests and visions of their participants. Community-based learning experiences that incorporate service learning principles complement primary health care and provide a means for nursing educators to better prepare future nurses (Kataoka-Yahiro, Cohen, Yoder, & Canham, 1998)

- to care for the community's health;
- to emphasize primary care;
- to practice prevention;
- to promote healthy lifestyles;
- to understand the role of the physical environment;
- to participate in a culturally diverse society;
- to fulfill the needs of the underserved vulnerable populations;
- to ensure cost effective care;
- to involve patients, families, and communities in the decision making process; and
- to create autonomous nurse-managed care.

When service learning combines with community-based nursing education, a mutually reciprocal partnership is born. It is a futuristic partnership that will enable professional nursing to be at the forefront in health care delivery systems and a key leader in responding to the health problems that face our nation now and in the future.

REFERENCES

Cookfair, J. M. (1996). *Nursing care in the community* (2nd ed.). St. Louis, MO: Mosby.

Kataoka-Yahiro, M., Cohen, J., Yoder, M., & Canham, D. (1998). A learning-service community partnership model for pediatric student experiences. *Nursing and Health Care Perspectives*, 19(6), 274–277.

Henry, J. A. (1999). Seeing the community through a new lens. *Connections*. Richmond, VA: School of Nursing, Medical Center of Virginia Campus; Virginia Commonwealth University.

McWilliam, C. L., Desai, K., & Greig, B. (1997). Bridging town and gown: Building research partnerships between community-based professional providers and academia. *Journal of Professional Nursing*, 13(5), 307–315.

Richards, R., Grace, G., & Henry, R. (1991). *Community partnerships*: A *Kellogg initiative in health professionals education*. Battle Creek, MI: W.K. Kellogg Foundation.

Shoultz, J., & Amundson, M. J. (1998). Nurse educators' knowledge of primary health care: Implications for community-based education, practice, and research. *Nursing and Health Care Perspectives*, 19(3), 115–119.

Shugars, E., O'Neil, E. H., & Bader, J. (Eds.). (1991). *Healthy America: Practitioners for 2005, an agenda for action for U.S. health professional schools.* Durham, NC: Pew Health Professions Commission.

U.S. Department of Health and Human Services. (2000). *Healthy People* 2010 (Conference Ed., 2 volumes).Washington, DC: Author.

World Health Organization. (1978). *Primary health care: Report of the International Conference on Primary Health Care,* Alma-Ata, USSR. Geneva, Switzerland: Author.

World Health Organization Study Group. (1986). *Regulatory mechanisms for nursing training and practice: Meeting primary health care needs* (WHO Tech. Rep. Ser. 738). Geneva, Switzerland: Author.

CHAPTER

2

SERVICE LEARNING: ENHANCING EDUCATION, PRACTICE, AND RESEARCH

Dr. Gail P. Poirrier

The incorporation of service learning concepts in nursing education recon-ceptualizes the relationship between theory and practice while adding a higher level of thinking and application that leads to reciprocal learning in nontraditional environmental and community settings. In addition, service learning sets the stage for a lifelong commitment to development of civic duty, social awareness and engagement, and the nurse educator role responsibili-ties closely affiliated within the profession of nursing in meeting the health care needs of society.

Henderson and Nite (1978) viewed nursing as a service derived from the universal human needs of people with health teaching, health promotion, and prevention of disease as major functions of nursing practice. Florence Nightin-gale viewed her work in nursing as her single most important contribution to society and described nursing as an expression of her citizenship and religion. She was the first to use health statistics as leverage in effecting health legis-lation changes in England and other parts of the British Empire. Since the Nightingale era, many other nursing leaders have continued to shape nursing, with emphasis on the psychosocial aspects of nursing and seeing nursing as significant in changing the social order (Woodham-Smith, 1950). Today, nurs-ing remains both a practice- and service-oriented profession, with service be-ing tightly webbed in the philosophy of nursing.

If the discipline of nursing is to continue its major role in the delivery of health care in our society, the education of nurses must change (Shoultz & Amundson, 1998). As nursing practice embodies more community-based, community-focused health care demands from the public and health care delivery systems, nursing education must ensure that nurse educators are prepared to revise nursing curricula and teaching strategies in terms of community-based primary health care knowledge and skills. As mentioned in the previous chapter, several other national and global initiatives have

5

addressed the education of health professionals as a key factor related to the transition to a primary health care system (Richards, Grace, & Henry, 1991; Shugars, O'Neil, & Bader, 1991). Academicians are often consumed within their institutional boundaries and research agendas and have been accused of not connecting with and reacting to "real world" societal issues. Service learning can help academicians to finally prove that they can respond to communities and make a difference by the very nature of their expertise through education, research, and practice (McWilliam, Desai, & Greig, 1997).

The practice of nursing is based on several accepted theoretical frameworks that are reflective of man, health, and society. Such theoretical frameworks, which can be applied to service learning, include (1) the general systems theory, (2) Maslow's human needs theory, and (3) the holistic model (Hale, 1997). Service learning not only complements the practice of nursing but also provides for transition to primary health care in a nontraditional learning environment and community. Today's nurses deliver care in multiple settings across traditional and nontraditional boundaries. With new practice sites and responsibilities for nurses, the future holds promise that this trend will continue in health care (Meservey, 1995; Faller, Dowell, & Jackson, 1995). Nursing education must embrace service learning as a sound educational means to better educate and prepare future nurses for the society in which we live. Service learning strategies offer unique learning experiences integrating classroom instruction and community service with knowledge development. Incorporating service learning across nursing curricula is a win-win strategy for nursing education and practice.

To prepare nurses for general practice settings, nursing education has traditionally employed habitual types of teaching and learning methodologies, such as didactic presentation in a classroom followed by application activities in a lab or clinical setting such as a hospital, client's home, or community/public health clinic. Since the concepts of service are already entrenched in both nursing practice and nursing education, nursing faculty should not have difficulty reprogramming learning methods that expand beyond the established and dominant experiential mode (Ciaccio & Walker, 1998).

Service learning provides for "real life" experiences that are meaningful not only to nursing students but also to the individuals, families, and groups within an environment and community. Nursing students actually learn to serve while serving to learn. The *unique worth of service learning* activities is the additional focus on building

- citizenship,
- civic pride,
- new values and skills,
- cultural diversity,
- community partnerships,
- respect for humankind,
- knowledge of community resources, and
- continued commitment to societal needs.

Critical thinking skills are sharpened, interpersonal and communication skills are enhanced, and innovative interventions are developed and implemented during the service learning process to help communities meet their health care needs. Service learning is active and participatory, which has been quantified as learning that is more readily retained (Hill, 1985; Watson, Church, & Darville, 1996).

Students view service learning as "real learning" and important academic work that has meaning. Service learning activities give students a sense of achievement and purpose as they make contributions to their communities by touching lives. In essence, their whole educational experience is enriched.

For faculty, service learning activities can liven the teaching environment. In addition, faculty gain awareness of the community that is served by the educational institution and can more readily connect with the outreach or service mission of the parent institution. Service learning serves as a mechanism to further bridge the gap between education (faculty) and practice (practitioners). Practice sees education as having a real world sense of societal need, and faculty who engage in service learning have a sense of knowing that they are congruent with societal need.

Research is essential to advancing the practice and profession of nursing. To advance research efforts, educators must stay abreast of changes, identify gaps in the knowledge base, and initiate research projects. Service learning, which provides students with an opportunity to critically examine civic and social responsibilities of nursing education, is an early introduction to the need to self-educate in relation to a discipline's knowledge base. Service learning activities assist students to clearly look at societal issues in relation to health, to critically reflect about society's needs and one's responsibility to one's community, to explore alternative solutions to problems, and to share ideas with peers, communities, and other audiences. All of these are important steps to "using research" in practice and are emphasized by the American Nurses Association (ANA, 1995) as standards of performance.

The community partnerships created via service learning presents nursing faculty with a resourceful playground for meaningful research. Service learning brings new research interests and ideas to nursing faculty and exposes faculty to many societal problems and new health care needs. This exposure can serve as a catalyst to investigation and inquiry, resulting in future nursing journal publications, research endeavors, and a stronger research and knowledge base for the discipline of nursing.

REFERENCES

American Nurses Association (ANA). (1995). *Standards of clinical nursing practice*. Washington, DC: Author.

Ciaccio, J., & Walker, G. C. (1998). Nursing & service learning: The Kobyashi Maru. *Nursing and Health Care Perspectives*, 19(4), 175–177.

Faller, H. S., Dowell, M. A., & Jackson, M. A. (1995). Bridge to the future: Nontraditional clinical settings, concepts, and issues. *Journal of Nursing Education, 34,* 344–349.

Hale, A. (1997). Service-learning within the nursing curriculum. *Nurse Educator, 22*(2), 15–18.

Henderson, V., & Nite, G. (1978). *Principles and practice of nursing* (6th ed.). New York: Macmillan.

Hill, P. (1985, October). *The rationale for learning communities.* Speech transcript from the Inaugural Conference on Learning Communities of the Washington Center for Undergraduate Education, Evergreen State College, WA.

McWilliam, C. L., Desai, K., & Greig, B. (1997). Bridging town and gown: Building research partnerships between community-based professional providers and academia. *Journal of Professional Nursing, 13*(5), 307–315.

Meservey, P. M. (1995). Fostering collaboration in a boundaryless organization. *Nursing and Health Care: Perspectives on Community, 16,* 234–236.

Richards, R., Grace, G., & Henry, R. (1991). *Community partnerships: A Kellogg initiative in health professional's education.* Battle Creek, MI: W.K. Kellogg Foundation.

Shoultz, J., & Amundson, M. J. (1998). Nurse educators' knowledge of primary health care: Implications for community-based education, practice, and research. *Nursing and Health Care Perspectives, 19*(3), 115–119.

Shugars, E., O'Neil, E. H., & Bader, J. (Eds.). (1991). *Healthy America: Practitioners for 2005, an agenda for action for U.S. health professional schools.* Durham, NC: Pew Health Professions Commission.

Watson, J. B., Church, C., & Darville, S. (1996). *Training manual for eldercare service-learning faculty: Eldercare learn and serve project.* Nacogdoches, TX: Stephen F. Austin State University.

Woodham-Smith, C. (1950). *Florence Nightingale, 1820–1910.* London: Constable & Co.

From Plato's Cave to Civic Purpose: The Making of a Service Learning Program

Dr. Gary Marotta

The Meeting

It always begins with a meeting. Somewhere, in the community outside the campus, in the halls of the legislature, among students in the union, between faculty in a lounge, over a staff conference table, somebody is possessed by an idea so powerful that it commands its possessor to gain it a hearing, to test it, to ascertain whether the idea can come to life. It helps if the possessor has influence or credibility; it helps even more if the idea can be articulated lucidly and persuasively. That combination of credibility and lucidity can be compelling, even in the face of resistance.

The meeting was to be in my office; the sign on the door reads *Vice President for Academic Affairs*. My appointment book told me that the vice president for university advancement was scheduled to see me about service learning and AmeriCorp. My mind was on strengthening faculty research, gaining accreditation for professional programs, recruiting top scholars, core curriculum and canon debates, affirmative action goals, achieving enrollment targets and improving student performance, developing doctoral programs, and preparing a case for an endowed chair for consideration by a benefactor. Funds also needed to be secured for the startup of new laboratories and studios, for upgrading computing infrastructure, and for library acquisitions. Proposals directed to NEH, NSF, NIH, and NASA were awaiting my study and signature. My calendar also told me I had a meeting with the Faculty Senate that afternoon. Service learning and AmeriCorp were not on the radar. I didn't even know what the terms meant.

The meeting was not, as I had hoped, brief and informational. The vice president was possessed by the idea. He explained service learning and AmeriCorp funding. He spoke of meaning in students' lives, of connectivity between classrooms and community, and of an engaged, socially active university. The university was already committed to regional economic development and diversity, he reminded me. Let's also engage the students; let's build community and be whole, he argued. The vice president for university advancement came out of the student affairs area; he had an acute feeling for student development and community needs. He was a populist, and now he was armed with a philosophy acquired at Columbia University's Teachers College. John Dewey still lived, revivified by Benjamin Barber.

I had arrived at the University of Southwestern Louisiana a few years earlier. Our charge was to move it from a comprehensive regional university to a research II university; we had achieved doctoral II status and were on our way to doctoral I ranking. The projected next step, research II, would be very difficult and protracted. My mind and energy were focused on the academic plan, the deans and faculty were driving hard, and the president kept scarce dollars moving into academics and research. This was the last thing I needed (a new initiative that might reallocate resources and dissipate energy). I reminded my colleague of our charge to be nationally competitive. Besides, I confided, I was suspicious of initiatives that diverted attention away from study and academic achievement. There were too many institutions of almost higher learning that masked academic deficiency with social commitment. I wanted to stay in Plato's cave.

Despite my firm protestations, my colleague sensed my vulnerability. I liked his idea, and he knew it. I had come from a proletarian neighborhood in Brooklyn, New York, where we subscribed to the same ideals of democratic social justice. We wanted to mix with the laity in the work of building a better world, or at least a better Louisiana. After all, what was the purpose of education? And, for that matter and in particular, what was the purpose of education at a public university in a poor state?

Plato would not have Socrates suggest to his pupils that their learning be confined to the Lyceum. I knew of the ideal of Athenian citizenship from Pericle's oration and understood the Greek word *paideia*, the relationship between public culture and learning, civility itself. My education and ideals conspired to predispose me to my colleague's polished pitch. He needed my support—he could not carry the idea without academic affairs—and he won it.

I conceded to seeing the light. It was a good idea, it was consistent with the university mission, it would establish powerful institutional partnerships, and it would be vital to the development of our students. We met again to think through the idea further and agreed to bring it to University Council. We planned our presentation strategy.

THE DECISION

The University Council consists of the vice presidents and several senior staff members. It is the policy making group for the university. The vice president for academic affairs sets the agenda and at once mediates and participates in the discussions; the president listens, asks questions, and makes the decisions. Getting to *yes* is difficult.

The vice president for university advancement made the principal presentation. He reviewed the purposes and principles of service learning and outlined its advantages. The vice president for academic affairs supported the initiative and argued that it reinforced the academic and research direction of the university. As the institution moved toward doctoral I status, he argued, it is essential to reaffirm undergraduate learning as well as to improve retention and graduation rates. Ernest Boyer's *Scholarship Reconsidered*, Derik Bok's *Beyond the Ivory Tower*, and Benjamin Barber's *An Aristocracy of Everyone* were marshaled to make the case. We discussed a short speech by President Clinton, "National Service—Now," which appealed for congressional support for AmeriCorp legislation. The vice president for student affairs endorsed the initiative. A Benedictine-trained social activist, he argued that parallel support for economic development and social engagement would make the university distinctive; the initiative could attack deep social problems in the community, bond Black and White citizens and students alike, and invest town-and-gown with a sense of community.

We were moving toward yes until the discussion turned into a debate over financing. We offered a preliminary budget, but it was judged soft. What will the initiative really cost and can we afford it? I was not prepared to divert further resources from the academic plan, and neither was the president. In fact, the president embodied the dilemma of the council: two good principles, the strengthening of the university and financial accountability, collided. That would mean no. Budget always trumps idealism.

But the president, long committed to public service, agreed that the two vice presidents would develop a plan. The plan must identify the organization and scope of service learning and must incorporate the precise nature of the public partnership; and its approval would be contingent upon gaining AmeriCorp grant support along with other external funding, with university commitments limited to in-kind and matching funds. The plan also must win the support of the Student Government Association, the Faculty Senate, and the Academic Council, which consisted of the deans of the colleges. So, it was neither a yes nor a no, but an amber light; the yes or no would be triggered by whether the contingencies were met. And the funding proposal would not be released without its budget scrutinized by the president.

THE PLAN

Now we knew the rules. Everything, all or nothing, depended on the plan. The two vice presidents invited a third partner to join the team. The chair of the Department of Sociology and Anthropology was selected because of his knowledge of experiential education, his prominent record of service to community associations and government agencies, and his respect among colleagues as scholar, teacher, and administrator. An inventory of existing university experiential courses, including internships, practicums, and student teaching, was assembled. The team developed a strategy to gain support and to test the terms of support. The vice president for academic affairs would work with the Faculty Senate and the Academic Council. The vice president for university advancement would work with the dean of students to gain support from the Student Government Association and also would work with the head of the department to identify community projects and to develop the external funding proposals.

After consultative sessions with the several constituency groups, the team defined specific principles for service learning:

- Student participation would be voluntary.
- Student participants would command superior grade point averages. Faculty participation would be voluntary.
- Faculty participants would be recognized for consideration for tenure, promotion, and annual merit increases.
- Appropriate credit courses, already extant, would be used to prepare students for service learning and to offer service learning experiences.
- Service learning projects would be invited by the community, and the community would be decisive in identifying project priorities.
- The program would be assessed regularly in accordance with the university outcome-assessment procedure.

The team searched the literature for a guiding pedagogy for service learning. The most succinct statement that captured our attention came from J. C. Kendall's (1990) *Combining Service and Learning*:

> . . . service learning is a philosophy of education which emphasizes active, engaged learning with the goal of social responsibility. . . it is reciprocal learning, dynamic and interactive. . . which suggests mutuality in learning between the student and the community with whom he or she is actively engaged. (pp. 22–23)

The principles embedded here were later made explicit in the program, its literature, and its formal agreements with faculty and students.

Perhaps the most exciting, complex, and rigorous work of all involved the development of community partnerships and the research behind the identification of projects. This work was done by the vice president for university advancement, members of his staff, and the head of the Department of Sociology and Anthropology. Through them, the university secured the active support of parish ("county" for the rest of the United States) and city governments. In fact, the director of community planning for the city and the director of the nonprofit volunteer center joined the partnership development group; their resources, knowledge, and contacts proved invaluable.

A sophisticated study of the city's Community Development Block Grant (CDBG) area was conducted in association with community groups and leaders. The study defined projects with precision, replete with goals, logistical plans, schedules, and budgets. Such research-based project planning became characteristic of the service learning program, and much of the program's success is attributed to its research orientation.

The organizational plan called for an administrative unit, the Service Learning Center, to be staffed by a director and secretary and to be led by a dean—the dean of community service. The dean would be assisted by two large groups—the Service Learning Council and the Advisory Committee. The Service Learning Council is composed of faculty representatives from participating academic departments and staff from key administrative units and is responsible for developing service learning within the university. The Advisory Committee, composed of permanent external partners, includes representatives from the parish, the city's department of community development, the city housing authority, the parish public school system, and the regional volunteer center (which connects the university to over 190 nonprofit associations involved in nonpolitical community projects). The council and the committee are connected and coordinated by the dean and his staff. They meet jointly, as needed, to develop specific projects and come together, along with students and community groups, in the annual Service Learning Conference.

The dean of community service reports to both the vice president for academic affairs (for academic coordination) and the vice president for university advancement (for community and government relations), corresponding to the Service Learning Council and the Advisory Committee, respectively. Thus, the dean of community service has high level access and support, clearly identifying the Service Learning Center as a priority university initiative. Now, dual reporting patterns usually do not work, but this one made sense. Moreover, the head of the Department of Sociology and Anthropology was appointed dean, and we subscribed to the same values and system of organization. We also bonded by going through the process together.

The plan (Savoie, 1995; Savoie and Palmer, 2000) for service learning was promulgated, along with its role, scope, mission, and governance. The Service Learning Center was provided with offices, infrastructure, and budget. The plan won support from the Faculty Senate, the Academic Council, and the Student Government Association. The organization was approved by the university president and appropriate governing boards. The university's proposal for AmeriCorp funding was successful, augmented by private funding from the Junior League and area businesses.

The work of the Service Learning Center was implemented, and its success has been astounding. It has become a model for the State of Louisiana and is praised by community and political leadership. It is strongly encouraged by the lieutenant governor—she visits the center; meets with students, faculty, and staff; and has commended its authentic "culture of service." The Louisiana Service Commission, which competitively allocates AmeriCorp block grant funds from the federal government, reports to the lieutenant governor. It is especially important to keep external leaders informed about and involved in the program; their support is essential.

At the end of each academic year, the center sponsors a major, full-day service learning conference, rich with workshops. Morale is always high. In 1996, after its first year of operation, I introduced the keynote speaker, Dr. Benjamin Barber, Walt Whitman Chair of Political Science at Rutgers University. He is, in our judgment, the visionary and theoretician of the service learning movement in American higher education. He spoke eloquently on "Community Service in a Democracy: Philanthropy or Citizenship?"

I turned to my colleague on the stage, formerly the vice president for university advancement and now commissioner of higher education for the Board of Regents of Louisiana. We met the eyes of the dean of community service. We didn't speak; we smiled. We knew it was all worth it. Later, after the keynote address, Dr. Barber sought us out to get direction to the place where he would be giving a workshop. He was happy to be in French Louisiana, on his way to the Bastile room! Ah, more prisoners to liberate!

CONCLUSION

Early in my career as a university administrator, while serving as executive assistant to the chancellor of Long Island University, I found myself in the extraordinary circular office of William Zeckendorf, Sr., chairman of the university's Board of Trustees and legendary New York real estate developer. Among other things, he owned the Empire State Building and put the deal together to build the United Nations in New York City; I. M. Pei was then the firm's exclusive architect. (Donald "The Donald" Trump, when starting out in the industry, looked to Zeckendorf as his model and idol.) I was young then, and Zeckendorf must have sensed my lack of experience. He explained that he would tell me all I needed to know about administration in four minutes. You have to know about meetings and plans, he said. As for meetings, prepare for them, get through them, and follow up immediately. As for plans, he said there are "the three z's: organize, deputize, and supervise." Okay, so he wasn't a world-class speller, but he knew what he was talking about. If something goes wrong, he explained, ask yourself what you failed to do: Did you fail to put the appropriate organization in place? Did you fail to put the right person in charge? Did you fail to supervise properly?

Administrative and university support for service learning at the University of Southwestern Louisiana, now the University of Louisiana at Lafayette, was sufficient to permit the program to start, to grow, and to develop. The organization and the person in charge of the program were right for its success, a nice praxis. Because of its success, the question of supervision has never arisen. The dean's status, reporting to two vice presidents, invested the program with clout and visibility. From the very start, there was "buy-in" from all the principal constituents; they took ownership. The dean himself was committed to the program. He believed, most of all, in its purpose, its guiding philosophy, and its meaning for the university, for its students and faculty, and for the community. Thus, a project that began at the top built grassroots support. This, the key to its success, is the doing of the dean; leadership and management are essential in building loyal, widespread support among faculty and students and community. It is also very important for the morale of those dedicated to the program to know that it commands the support of the senior administration (Holland, 1997).

For the University of Louisiana at Lafayette, service learning is reconciling the two contesting models within the university—the purist model, with its call for ivory tower insularity and learning for its intrinsic reward; and the vocational model, with its call for assimilation into the purpose of the larger society and learning for its external reward. The reconciliation is achieved through the "culture of service" integral to service learning. This culture of service daily insinuates itself into the very life of the university. It redefines faculty and student roles and responsibilities in service, teaching, and research, and it integrates the university into its community based on the freshly articulated civic values of the university itself (Palmer, 1997). "Does the university have a civic mission?" asks Benjamin Barber (1989):

> Of course, for it is a civic mission: the cultivation of free community; the creation of a democracy of words (knowledge) and a democracy of deeds (the democratic state). Perhaps it is time to stop complaining about the needs of society and worrying about the fate of the canon and despairing over the inadequacy of students. . . Perhaps the time is finally here to start thinking about what it means to say that community is the beginning and the end of education: its indispensable condition, its ultimate object. And time then, if we truly believe this, to do something about it in words and in deeds. (p. 72)

Such is the belief of Jefferson and Hamilton, of Walt Whitman, and of William James. It is a profoundly American democratic belief. You have to believe, as Barber suggests, if we are to legitimatize the public purpose of the university in American life and culture. It is nothing less than *paideia*: the university does not only *have* a civic mission—it *is* a civic mission. Let us stay with Plato, but let us move out of the cave and into the world of urban, rural, and suburban America, where we live—and where we can make a difference.

REFERENCES

Barber, B. R. (1989). The civic mission of the university. *Kettering Review*, 72.

Holland, B. (1997). Analyzing institutional commitment to service: A model of key organizational factors. *Michigan Journal of Community Service Learning*.

Kendall, J. C. (1990). *Combining service and learning*, Vol. I. Raleigh, NC: National Society for Internships and Experiential Education.

Palmer, C. E. (1997). *The development of a culture of service at a mid-sized university: Some sociological reflections.* Paper presented at the annual meeting of the Mid-South Sociological Association, Huntsville, AL.

Savoie, E. J. (1995). *The development of a collaborative effort to establish a university-based service learning program*. Unpublished doctoral dissertation, Teacher's College, Columbia University.

Savoie, E. J., & Palmer, C. E. (2000). *Developing a university-based service learning program*. Paper presented at the Sociology of Education Session at the annual meeting of the Southwestern Sociological Association, Galveston, TX.

SERVICE LEARNING: A CONCEPTUAL OVERVIEW

Dr. Charles E. Palmer
Dr. E. Joseph Savoie

Curricular-based service learning exploded upon the higher education academic scene in the 1980s and 1990s and continues to gather force and momentum as we move into the new millennium. Books, journals, articles, papers, Web sites, list servs, conferences, retreats, workshops, organizations, and planning sessions continue to proliferate and advance service learning across the country. Service learning has gained a following of administrators, faculty members, staff members, and students from colleges and universities of all sorts and from citizens from all strata of society. This brief chapter will provide a conceptual overview of service learning. Such an overview is considered important because there remains in some quarters confusion about the exact nature of service learning and the various forms, shapes, and dimensions it takes on campuses throughout the United States today.

EXPERIENTIAL EDUCATION, SERVICE, AND SERVICE LEARNING

Contrasted with a passive, listening-to-lectures, sitting-in-a-classroom type of education (whether in a preuniversity or university setting), experiential education is active, hands-on, interactionally engaged, and sensually complex. Experiential education provides students the opportunity to gain new information, to test theory with reality-based applications, to be involved in practical demonstrations, and to evaluate the efficacy of various educational perspectives and approaches. Experiential learning means learning through experience. Experiential learning, however, can be done without being connected to a service ethic just as service can be done without being connected to a learning ethic, experiential or otherwise. Internships, for example, are

17

experiential in nature as are various types of "cooperative education" arrangements where students work for companies while studying and pursuing their degrees. Interns and co-op students, while engaged in experiential learning, may be focused clearly on problem solving, skills acquisition, and training for future employment. Service to others may never enter this experiential/ professional equation. Service in these instances may actually be seen as a hindrance or impediment to the successful completion of a preprofessional internship.

Service in terms of pure service to others is commonplace on today's university campuses. At universities one will find organizations, chapters, groups, and individuals dedicated to making the community a better place in which to live. Service can be a major theme or a minor component of student-led, faculty-sponsored groups. Service may be a requirement of membership or merely a suggested component. University students are often solicited to serve as volunteers in the community and to support events, initiatives, and movements that require warm bodies *en masse*. Some universities, for example, "require" students to perform community service before graduation, but the service is not curriculum based and is not directed toward specific learning objectives. Likewise, with numerous student organizations, students may learn something as a result of their service, but the learning may be serendipitous, disjointed, eclectic, unfocused, and unconnected.

Curricular-based service learning connects specific educational objectives to experientially based service performances and activities within the community. Barbara Jacoby (1996) points out that service learning in higher education is performed differently because of distinctly different institutional missions and traditions. Some universities embrace service learning as a philosophy, some as part of a spiritual mission, some as part of a commitment to "citizenship, civic responsibility, and participatory democracy," and some "ground their service-learning programs in community partnerships and public problem solving" (Jacoby, 1996, p. 17). Regardless of the specific institutional mission or tradition influencing the character of service learning, Jacoby (1996, p. 5) identifies four cardinal components in their definition of service learning, which is the definition adopted at the University of Louisiana at Lafayette. Service learning must (1) be experiential in nature, (2) allow students to engage in activities that address human and community needs via structured opportunities for student learning and development, (3) be reflective, and (4) embrace the concept of reciprocity between the service learner and the persons being served. J. C. Kendall (1990) explains that service learning, "is a philosophy of education which emphasizes active, engaged learning with the goal of social responsibility. . . . which suggests mutuality in learning between the student and the community with whom he or she is actively engaged" (pp. 22–23).

William Ramsey and Robert Sigmon are credited with the pioneering work through which the term *service learning* emerged (Jacoby, 1996, p. 12). First working at the Oak Ridge Institute of Nuclear Studies (later changed to Oak Ridge

Associated Universities) and then at the Southern Regional Education Board housed in Atlanta, Georgia, William Ramsey said that the term *service learning* resulted from a meeting specifically called to name the activity that results from academic internships that are connected to community development (C. E. Palmer and W. Ramsey, personal communication, February 9, 2000 and March 24, 2000).

According to Mark Langseth and Marie Troppe (1997), "Over the last 10 years, American higher education has made great strides in combining community service with academic, civic, and career development in students—or what is now commonly referred to as service-learning" (p. 37). Langseth and Troppe (1997) take the position that to produce significant social change, ". . . we must be willing to expand our definition of service beyond charitable volunteerism and engage with students and community members in multifaceted approaches to addressing social challenges" (p. 42).

The breadth of actions performed under the rubric of service learning and the amount of agreement about the crucial elements of service learning are critically addressed by Kevin Mattson and Margo Shea (1997) when they state, "Practitioners dispute. . . which principles of practice are essential, and how to differentiate between service-learning and volunteer community service, internships, cooperative education, career training, experiential education and participatory action research. These . . . debates lose sight of service-learning's dynamic, unpredictable and context-driven learning processes" (p. 16).

Many service learning proponents advocate service learning as a means of increasing participatory democracy, developing and improving citizenship, and producing informed, socially responsible, and energetic new community leaders. The writings of John Dewey (1916), Derek Bok (1982), and Benjamin Barber (1992), to name only a few, call for educational practice and institutional outreach to be directed toward the amelioration of social problems. Thus, service learning is a major vehicle to be used in combating social ills in the community.

In an essay that criticizes service learning as being too conservative in orientation to bring about any real social transformation, Tony Robinson (1999) contends that "the structural roots of problems" (p. 129) are being neglected. Robinson contends that ". . . political organizing, entailing an action-oriented critique of society and politics, is anathema to today's service-learning proponents" (p. 129).

Thus, service learning enjoys praise from some quarters, indifference from some, and criticism from yet others. When service learning is touted as the major way to educate today's university student, the major way to meet an institution's outreach mission, and the major way to solve social problems within the community—it is understandable that some would be unimpressed with service learning's potential. However, when service learning is used as an experientially based pedagogy within higher education to bring excitement and vitality to the classroom, to assist community members in need while at the same time learning from them, and to provide students with information and experiences through which to engage in critical reflection about society's needs and one's responsibility to one's community—then many become and remain impressed with service learning. In the following section we will provide a few examples of courses that meet these criteria at the University of Louisiana at Lafayette.

EXAMPLES OF SERVICE LEARNING COURSES

One service learning course at the University of Louisiana at Lafayette (hereafter, UL Lafayette) is a two-semester, six-hour sociology course (SOCI 391, 392) required of all members of the UL Lafayette AmeriCorps Community Service Program. Approximately 30 students are selected each year as AmeriCorps members who are each required to put in 900 clock hours of service during a one-year period. Members tutor in inner-city schools, work to improve academic performance by assisting students with homework in a housing development education center, and serve as liaisons connecting those in need with services available within the community. AmeriCorps members are assisted with developing a "sociological imagination" by reading standard sociological works and by applying concepts and definitions to their real world AmeriCorps experience. Students reflect on their service in group sessions, in written assignments (for example, values clarification exercises), and during didactic exchanges with the professor about the social forces impacting the lives of those served. Members draw from their experiences to provide examples in class discussions and to connect constructs with practice.

Another service learning course at UL Lafayette is an industrial technology course (ITEC 356) called Construction Management. This course is designed to teach students how to manage construction processes ranging from procurement of supplies and equipment needed for a construction project to supervision of construction personnel. The course is experiential in nature because students in ITEC 356 become the managers of students in lower level introductory ITEC courses. The upper level students survey the lower level students as to their construction skills, experience, and knowledge levels. After assessing these traits, the ITEC 356 students then go into the community in search of a construction project needed by a charitable organization. This search involves interviewing directors of nonprofit organizations about potential construction projects, determining the feasibility of the project, and actually selecting a site at which to work. A recent project involved the works of approximately 70 ITEC students who patched and painted 13 soon-to-be dormitory rooms for homeless men. Students interacted with homeless men during the project. Class discussions of a reflective nature were held by the ITEC 356 students about such topics as management strategies, philanthropy within the business community (students had to approach various agencies for donations of supplies, equipment, and food for the work teams), and the role of the profit motive in the construction industry.

The UL Lafayette faculty who teach Interpersonal Communication classes and Group Communication classes have implemented service learning in all sections of these classes. Based upon the decision to provide students in these communication classes with "more relevant and broadening communication experiences than they typically receive in regular classes" (Rockwell, 1999, p. 101), students complete a minimum of 15 clock hours of service learning work in a local organization during the semester. With faculty assistance, each student selects, contacts, and meets with a supervisor at a social service organization within the community and arranges the service learning project. The project must help meet a need in the community and must allow students the opportunity to use their communication skills. Skills taught in these courses range from anxiety management to conflict management, from listening to problem solving to tolerance (Rockwell, 1999, p. 101). Before implementing the service learning component of this course, students practice their skills on one another in the classroom. They then go to nursing homes and children's homes and engage in a variety of community improvement projects. Students keep reflective journals and participate in structured class discussions about their projects. Evaluations of the service learning experiences are made and kept, and responses have been "overwhelmingly positive" (Rockwell, 1999, p. 102). Reciprocity in these courses is evidenced by student comments such as, "The feedback I received from other people allowed me to see myself in a different way," and "I had a chance to interact with people I don't normally associate with" (p. 102).

In another service learning course, Emergency Health Science (EHS), students could choose from a variety of projects designed by their professor to educate children about bike safety, about how to call 911 to report accidents, and about emergency procedures used by paramedics responding to distress calls. One team of service learning students traveled to an area school to share information with pupils in one class and was asked by the principal to spend the whole day interacting with the student body. EHS students assembled after their demonstrations to reflect on the importance of their activities and to see if they needed to alter their delivery based on feedback from the public school students.

As will be seen in other chapters in this book, nursing students and nursing faculty at UL Lafayette are in the forefront of the campus-wide service learning initiative. Nursing students are involved in community-based nursing education led by faculty members who have designed nursing curricula specifically in keeping with the tenets of service learning outlined by Jacoby (1996, p. 5).

CONCLUSIONS

Service learning has recently made great inroads in higher education in the United States. Service learning, in its various shades and forms, has enlivened the educational process, has helped meet community needs, and has introduced a reflective dimension to learning. It has engaged students, faculty, administrators, agency directors, and community leaders in meaningful dialogue and discourse. It has helped universities meet their public service and outreach missions and along the way has helped to dispel the "isolationist" view of higher education held by some. It has made significant, meaningful, and heartfelt impacts on many within the academy and within the community.

REFERENCES

Barber, B. R. (1992). *An aristocracy of everyone, the politics of education and the future of America.* New York: Oxford University Press.

Bok, D. (1982). *Beyond the ivory tower: Social responsibilities of the modern university.* Cambridge, MA: Harvard University Press.

Dewey, J. (1916). *Democracy and education.* New York: Macmillan.

Jacoby, B. (1996). *Service-learning in higher education: Concepts and practices.* San Francisco: Jossey-Bass.

Kendall, J. C. (1990). *Combining service and learning: A resource book for community and public service,* Vol. I. Raleigh, NC: National Society for Internships and Experiential Education.

Langseth, M., & Troppe, M. (1997). So what? Does service-learning really foster social change? In Corporation for National Service, *Expanding boundaries: Building civic responsibility within higher education,* Vol. 2 (pp. 37–42). Columbia, MD: Cooperative Education Association (in cooperation with the Corporation for National Service).

Mattson, K., & Shea, M. (1997). The selling of service-learning to the modern university: How much will it cost? In Corporation for National Service, *Expanding boundaries: Building civic responsibility within higher education,* Vol. 2 (pp. 12–19). Columbia, MD: Cooperative Education Association (in cooperation with the Corporation for National Service).

Robinson, T. (1999). Saving the world (but without doing politics): The strange schizophrenia of the service-learning movement. *Academic Exchange Quarterly, 3,* 128–133.

Rockwell, P. (1999). Developing communication skills through service learning. *Academic Exchange Quarterly, 3,* 101–102.

CREATING A UNIVERSITY-BASED SERVICE LEARNING PROGRAM: BENEFITS AND CHALLENGES

Dr. Charles E. Palmer
Dr. E. Joseph Savoie

INTRODUCTION

As with most institutions of higher education, the statement of purpose of the University of Louisiana (UL) at Lafayette, as it appears in the 1997–1999 *Undergraduate Bulletin* of the university (then named the University of Southwestern Louisiana), contains descriptive language embracing basic education and service roles:

> The University of Southwestern Louisiana is a comprehensive, coeducational, public institution of higher education offering bachelor's, master's and doctoral degrees. The University reaffirms as its primary purpose the examination, transmission, preservation, and extension of mankind's intellectual traditions. Thus, the University emphasizes teaching, learning, scholarship, and public service (University of Southwestern Louisiana, 1997, p. 15).

This statement contains the seeds around which several individuals have recently attempted to germinate, develop, and expand a service learning initiative at this institution of over 16,000 students, located in a Southwestern Louisiana city with a population of approximately 110,000. This chapter describes the processes involved in the creation of this service learning program.

The University of Louisiana at Lafayette traditionally has embraced the concepts of teaching, research, and service to the university. The faculty self-evaluation procedures and the merit evaluation procedures used at the

This work is a revised version of a paper presented at the Sociology of Education Session at the 1999 meetings of the Southwestern Sociological Association titled "Developing a university-based service-learning program" by E. J. Savoie and C. E. Palmer.

university are designed to record one's efforts and accomplishments in these core areas of job performance. Many faculty members have contributed their time and efforts to the community *pro bono* in order to satisfy the university's requirement for community service and to assist community agencies in their roles of improving the quality of life of the area. These faculty efforts have included research consultancies, board memberships, volunteer activities, group memberships, and various charitable acts. Faculty members have also designed internships, field experiences, experiential learning opportunities, cooperative work placements, and other modes of community- or organization-based student involvement. In the 100-year history of the university, countless hours of public service have occurred as a result of the required and volunteer activities of faculty members, and due to the educational requirements and personal proclivities of students. Within the past six years, however, activities have occurred that attempt to bring a new dimension to the existing public service role of the university and to bring university efforts more in line with the national trend of expanded service learning. This chapter chronicles the brief history of the service learning movement at UL Lafayette.

THE BEGINNING

In the fall of 1993, the University Council, UL Lafayette's executive management team, began to discuss the need for the university to promote the development of civic responsibility and to broaden the social awareness of its students. In February 1994, the second author of this chapter (then vice president for university advancement at UL Lafayette) participated in a teleconference introducing AmeriCorps, a new federal domestic service program with a higher education component, and attended a conference sponsored by the Partnership for Service Learning, a consortium of universities that promote the use of service learning courses on college campuses. Concluding that the development of service learning courses utilizing the AmeriCorps program as the basis of the effort could meet the university's goals, a presentation proposing such an effort was made to and accepted by the University Council on February 28, 1994. The president of the university pledged support of the effort to both address social conditions in the community and to encourage the development of civic responsibility in students. He committed to providing staff time, university facilities, and public endorsement. In keeping with his conservative management philosophy, however, he expected direct funding of the program to come from grants and other external sources.

Research into Community Needs

Based upon advice and suggestions of a coordinating committee assembled to broaden the university outreach program, and in keeping with the focus of recently acquired grants from the Corporation for National Service, the East Simcoe Housing Development in Lafayette, Louisiana, was designated as a targeted service area. In order to implement an effective collaborative program of social action within this area, research was done in the community about the needs of the residents. Triangulated methodologies were employed and involved interviews of community leaders and influentials, a door-to-door survey of residents in the city's Community Development Block Grant (CDBG) area (including the East Simcoe Housing Development), a focus group meeting with CBDG residents, and a survey of and interviews with social service agency directors. By March 15, 1995, 51 separate data-gathering and planning events occurred involving numerous issues about community needs, faculty and student participation in service learning, implementation of grants, and collaboration with governmental agencies, service agencies, and residents and children of the targeted service area (Savoie, 1995, pp. 100–114).

The consensus derived from these activities was that we should direct our efforts toward the priority area of education and that we should concentrate on school success issues within our CDBG target area. We structured our 1995 AmeriCorps grant application around the concepts of tutoring, mentoring, and conflict resolution within selected schools within the central city and incorporated into our proposal an administrative structure at UL Lafayette through which service learning would be advanced. We were successful in our grant application and to date have received five AmeriCorps operating grants. Our sixth grant proposal was submitted in December of 1999. The remainder of this chapter will describe the administrative structure we developed to oversee the AmeriCorps grants and to advance service learning at UL Lafayette. In addition, we will address some of the benefits of this university-based program and articulate some of the challenges faced by those involved.

Developing Service Learning

The administrative structure of the service learning initiative at UL Lafayette hinges upon continued external funding of the initiative. A section of a previously successful AmeriCorps grant application describes the connection between the grant and the development of service-learning at this university and presents the charge of the dean of community service, a position held by the first author of this paper.

> As evidence of its strong commitment to the ethic of service, community building, and meeting unmet needs through this grant, the University proposes to create the high ranking position of Dean of Community Service . . . The Dean will be charged with directing the "AmeriCorps Scholars of Acadiana" grant and with developing, enhancing, and coordinating campus activities related to the overall creation and maintenance of a culture of service on the campus. The Dean of Community Service will work to increase the number of students and faculty involved in general service-learning activities; will aid faculty in the development, perfection, and implementation of resources designed to increase the experiential service component of complete well-rounded comprehensive education; will serve as a university liaison and support

person for participating governmental, community, and business agencies involved in the service-learning initiative; will attempt with the assistance of interested faculty, to locate, cultivate, and obtain extramural funds for the enhancement of the University Service-Learning Center, and will have oversight authority for the daily operation, maintenance, and staffing of the University Service-Learning Center . . . The Dean of Community Service will report to the Vice President for Academic Affairs for academic coordination at the highest level and to the Vice President for University Advancement for community and governmental coordination. (University of Southwestern Louisiana, 1995, p. 12).

To advance the initiative of service learning mentioned in the above charge, we first had to arrive at a means of increasing the number of students and faculty involved in service learning activities. One perspective was to require all students to put in a specified number of hours doing community service and/or to enroll in a course with a required service learning component. After considerable discussion, it was decided that we would attempt a grassroots effort whereby we would encourage faculty to voluntarily develop service learning course components or service learning courses and encourage voluntary student involvement. Such encouragement would come from both the academic affairs and student affairs areas of campus.

The Service Learning Council

The mechanism developed to spread the service learning message across campus is the Service Learning Council. The formation of this council was introduced by the vice president for academic affairs and the dean of community service at a called meeting of all academic deans and department heads. At this meeting, we asked for university-wide support and answered questions about service learning, which ranged from the definition of the concept ("How is it different from my internship program?"), to issues about the appropriateness of requiring students to perform community service ("We're an intellectual institution, not a church"), to the use of service learning on campus to help meet our outreach and public service mission ("This appears to fit well the concept of the interactive university").

At this initial meeting, we asked that each department on campus identify a person to serve on the Service Learning Council and followed up with a memo specifying the duties of council members. Some of these duties are as follows:

1. Discuss ways to generate more service-learning activity within each discipline on campus.
2. Discuss common problems/successes with service learning courses, course modules, or course projects.
3. Discuss ways to integrate co-curricular student service (for example, volunteer activities of those in student service organizations or sororities/fraternities) into curricular-based service learning.

4. Share information about existing service learning programs operating at other universities.
5. Identify research opportunities and funding sources associated with university-based service learning programs.
6. Organize, support, and evaluate an annual UL Lafayette Service Learning Conference.
7. Develop Service Learning Council committees as needed to respond to service learning needs/issues on campus.
8. Discuss methods of involving community agencies, corporations, and groups in this service learning initiative.

The Service Learning Council has developed some devoted members who take their charge seriously. They have served as panelists at council meetings, have shared their plans to incorporate service learning into their own courses, and have reported on their efforts to interest their colleagues in the concept. There are a few areas on campus that have yet to embrace service learning, and the hesitancy takes several forms. Some resist the idea on ideological grounds, some resist it on the grounds that it interferes with accreditation demands, some say that it adversely impacts their discipline-based pedagogical plans, some say it takes too much time, and others are attempting to find ways to add service learning to their courses but have yet to find ways that satisfy their academic requirements. To date we have developed service learning courses or course components in 20 departments and offer 42 courses to over 600 students annually. The College of Nursing and Allied Health Professions accounts for approximately 250 of these students.

The Service Learning Center

The UL Lafayette Service Learning Center is located in the same rooms as the AmeriCorps program and is designed to be used for meetings of interested faculty and staff to discuss service learning. The center received initial support from the Junior League of Lafayette in the form of a $10,000 grant to be used to support the initiative and to support our first Service Learning Conference held on campus in 1996. The Service Learning Center has its own budgetary line in the form of a Restricted Account number and receives support from the Business Services Office and the Internal Auditor to manage the Restricted Account funds.

The center has been used to organize three Service Learning Conferences held on campus in 1996, 1997, and 1998. The conferences drew faculty, students, social service agency staff, school teachers, and members of the general public together for meetings at which cooperative arrangements were made to disseminate service learning into the community. The conferences featured keynote speakers and breakout sessions and workshops. We offered student-led sessions where students spoke about their experiences and encouraged other students to participate in service learning opportunities on campus. Likewise, we had faculty-led sessions where faculty members spoke of their experiences and encouraged other faculty to support the campus initiative. Other sessions were organized by service agency directors who espoused the benefits of having students serve in their agencies while other sessions featured recipients of assistance who spoke of the reciprocal roles recipients and providers play upon the service learning stage. Some sessions brought together faculty and agency representatives to work out the logistics of establishing university-agency partnerships and to listen to each other's concerns about issues of liability, ethics, philosophy, and work scheduling. Refreshments were provided at the conferences, and networking and socializing occurred during the breaks between conference sessions. Surveys demonstrated a positive evaluation of these conferences.

We have also participated with the College of Nursing and Allied Health Professions in an annual Health Resource Fair held on campus. Local agencies offering health services come to campus to make contact with faculty, students, and each other. During this one-day event, students discuss with agency representatives the possibility of volunteer placements, internship opportunities, service-learning opportunities, and so on. Some students from nursing as well as nonnursing areas are given "scavenger-hunt assignments" and are challenged to locate an agency or a program offering particular types of services to particular clientele.

Additional links with the social service community are also developed and sustained by active membership in the local Social Service Agency Network. We periodically host one of the monthly meetings of this organization. This meeting, held at our alumni center facilities, includes a presentation about service learning developments on campus and offers new agency members in attendance opportunities to participate with us in service learning activities as well as in other internship, practica, and field work courses offered at UL Lafayette. These activities and others keep the service learning initiative directly connected to the community.

BENEFITS AND CHALLENGES

Some of the challenges associated with the service learning initiative at UL Lafayette are to be seen in the context of our institution. Our university is a fairly large, state-supported public institution of higher learning located within a state often plagued with financial, health, and socioeconomic difficulties. Support for higher education is a constant battle, and our institution has seen its share of "lean" financial times. Resources are often inadequate to support a wide array of programs and activities. Service learning has to look to external funding sources for support and has to depend upon the goodwill and dedication of faculty members to voluntarily alter their courses to fit the service-learning mode. Lack of dedicated institutional support, while understandable, remains one of the major challenges we face.

Another challenge lies in convincing faculty members to adopt service learning as an effective pedagogical device. Change of any kind is often resisted. Adding service learning to a course is time consuming and involves some restructuring of traditional pedagogical formats. Field supervisors are often needed, and this adds a dimension outside collaboration that is alien to some faculty who are worried about issues of ethics and liability. Some faculty endorse service learning but cannot "make the stretch" to create a satisfactory service learning experience for their particular courses. The "hard sciences," as well as math, engineering, and geology, are hard-pressed to fit service learning into their academic arenas. Finally, some remain ideologically opposed to service learning because it smacks of "do-gooderism" or conservative civic indoctrination, or because it is seen as a passing academic fad. Finding the time and inclination to convincingly argue the case for service learning is also a tough duty for the dean of community service, Service Learning Council members, and other supportive administrators. Keeping the service learning initiative front and center, fresh, and invigorated is challenging in and of itself.

The benefits of service learning far outweigh the challenges. Some disciplines and some faculty are ready-made for service learning. With very little "stretching" required, service learning brightens, enlivens, recharges, and energizes some faculty members who look forward to the improved course evaluations that result from adding service learning to their teaching repertoire. Classroom discussions become more enjoyable because students have experiences they can bring to the table for discussion and often become more engaging as critical thinkers who pose interesting questions in class. Service learning students are connected to authentic educational experiences. They find service learning exciting. They learn from doing and enjoy a qualitatively different educational experience. Through their service projects they are able to ground their learning with practical experience. As much service learning is done in groups, students form friendship networks and rely upon each other for support and assistance. Students use service learning to improve and expand their resumes and often make contact with prospective employers while in the field completing their projects. Service learning adds value to students' educational experiences in numerous ways, not the least of which is a memorable shaping and molding of attitudes that will remain with them for a lifetime.

Faculty members, even though not directly compensated or specifically rewarded for their service learning involvement, indirectly benefit from such involvement. A sense of satisfaction accrues to those who successfully employ service learning as a teaching method. Those who are civic-minded feel they are doing their duty to produce like-minded students who become informed and active in government and community affairs as a result of a service learning inspired introduction to participatory democracy. Service learning experiences give faculty members material for writing grants, books (such as this one), professional papers, articles, and speeches. A sense of collegiality results from intra- and interdisciplinary activities among faculty who share the service learning journey. Those who feel an obligation to use their knowledge,

skills, and talents to improve the human condition take pride in the consequences of service learning. While not paramount in affecting merit raises,
some faculty satisfy their "service" requirements through service learning
activities.

Educational institutions are better able to meet their outreach and public
service roles when they nurture a cadre of faculty and students who work and
learn experientially within the community. Service learning is good public relations. The human condition is improved by the services performed by students whether these services are health related, educationally related, or related to improving the efficiency and effectiveness of social service agencies.
A service learning program is a mark of a vital institution that is connected to
its constituents in a humane and meaningful way. Service learning is a signal
of an "interactive" university and represents a value-added dimension of
higher education.

SUMMARY AND CONCLUSIONS

The University of Louisiana at Lafayette established a curricular-based service learning program in 1995. The effort was initiated by members of the university advancement sector who were quickly joined by the academic affairs
and student life sectors of the university. Having received a planning grant
from the Louisiana Service Commission in 1994, university personnel and
members of a community advisory committee engaged in research in the
community. This research showed a need to assist those living in the CDBG
area of the city in order to improve student performance and elevate overall
school success. Future Louisiana Service Commission/Corporation for National Service AmeriCorps grants allowed the creation of a funded service
learning program, which to date has supported over 150 AmeriCorps students
who have logged thousands of hours of direct service within the community.
An additional 600 students participate in service learning activities annually,
the majority of whom are nursing majors. Using federal AmeriCorps funds as a
springboard, the university developed a Service Learning Center, organized
and hosted three Service Learning Conferences, established an active 45-per-
son Service Learning Council, and received additional funding from the local
chapter of the Junior League to support service learning activities, and from
the Powell Group to buy supplies for our off-campus Education Center. We
have also benefitted from the proceeds of two invitational basketball tourna-
ments developed and sponsored by a local law firm.

We adopted a voluntary approach to the creation of service learning opportunities on campus, thinking that a grassroots movement would gain more
solid faculty and student support than would the mandating of service learning for all students. Mandating or requiring all students to engage in community service would be logistically problematic for a student body of 16,000
within a community of 110,000 and would not necessarily ensure a true serv-

ice learning academic experience. While the grassroots method may be slower than a system mandating service, we believe that the voluntary approach is more in line with the true character of higher education, academic freedom, and intellectual inquiry. We believe that the strides made using our approach testify to the acceptability of our strategy, even though we face a variety of challenges as outlined above. Nevertheless, we feel that we are well postured to make important advances in the coming semesters and that more and more students and faculty will join our ranks with academically sound, socially significant, and personally rewarding service learning agendas.

REFERENCES

Savoie, E. J. (1995). *The development of a collaborative effort to establish a university-based service learning program*: *A case study*. Unpublished doctoral dissertation, Teachers College, Columbia University.

University of Southwestern Louisiana. (1995). *AmeriCorps Scholars of Acadiana* (AmeriCorps State Grant Application). Lafayette, LA: University of Southwestern Louisiana.

University of Southwestern Louisiana. (1997). 1997–1999 *Undergraduate Bulletin*, Vol. 78, p. 15. Lafayette, LA: University of Southwestern Louisiana.

CHAPTER

INCORPORATING SERVICE LEARNING ACROSS THE NURSING CURRICULUM

Dr. Carolyn Delahoussaye

Incorporation of service learning into a nursing curriculum offers students the opportunity to become involved in partnerships with community organizations as a part of activities related to experiential courses. Through experiential learning and collaborative efforts that address community needs, students achieve a heightened sense of social responsibility and gain an increased awareness of current societal issues. Integrating theoretical learning and service learning better prepares students to become active and responsible members of our society within the context of their professional goals and achievements.

Public service is emphasized in the Statement of Purpose of the University of Louisiana at Lafayette, ". . . University is dedicated to achieving excellence in . . . public service . . . to develop scholars who will . . . improve the material conditions of humankind. . . ." Public service can be integrated into university curricula through the addition of service learning concepts and activities. The concept of service learning utilizing Jacoby's (1996) definition was introduced to university deans and department heads as a first step in expanding service learning activities within the university.

The service learning council was formed as a grassroots effort to begin to implement service learning across campus. University faculty and students and representatives from numerous community organizations were invited to attend a service learning conference to discuss the development of experiential education and the expansion of service learning opportunities throughout the community. Conference topics addressed needs, concerns, and outcomes of service learning for students, faculty, curriculum, and local agencies and organizations within the community.

In addition to promoting the annual service learning conferences, service learning council members were charged with expanding the number of service learning activities available to students within their disciplines. The dean and the department head for the Department of Nursing were in full support of integrating service learning into the nursing curriculum. Service is emphasized in the mission statement of the baccalaureate nursing program, which includes the goal ". . . to prepare leaders in professional nursing who are responsive to the health needs of diverse cultures through caring, integration of critical thinking, research-based practice, and technological advancements . . . actualized through . . . quality education, research, scholarship, and community service." The mission is actualized through the following goals for the program:

1. Provide a quality program of study that leads to a Bachelor of Science degree in Nursing for a diverse group of students.
2. Through implementation of principles of active learning, foster the development of critical thinking skills relevant to the discipline of nursing.
3. Prepare nurses who can assume leadership roles in the provision of quality, cost-effective health care to diverse populations.
4. Create an environment that is conducive to the advancement of nursing research, scholarship, and practice.
5. Balance the integration of emerging technologies with caring within the framework of professional nursing practice.

Although nursing is a service profession, the practice experiences of nursing students are not automatically categorized as service learning activities. Nursing faculty were given the opportunity to dialogue about how nursing clinical practice experiences might qualify as service learning activities for students. Four common elements must be present for a practicum experience to also be a service learning experience: (1) The learning experience meets a human need and/or solves a community problem. Faculty were able to agree that this element is present in all courses within the nursing curriculum that have a clinical practice component. The basis of nursing practice is the promotion of health and the prevention of illness through identification of human and community needs in a variety of settings. (2) The learning experience is experiential and fulfills the educational requirements of the course. Again, faculty discussion led to the identification of the clinical courses within the curriculum. All clinical courses are experiential; that is, students go to a practice setting and provide individuals and/or communities with hands-on nursing care that is based on course theory. (3) The learning experience is structured so that students and faculty participate in a health-related activity with community members within the context of reciprocity. The faculty dialogue about this element provided an opportunity for expanded awareness. It was obvious that the community members learned from the students, and it was also obvious that the students learned how to implement their professional roles with the community members. To more fully dimensionalize the element of reciprocity, the faculty dialogued about what the community taught each student that would enable the student to experience a greater sense of civic responsibility. They decided that the nursing curriculum courses in the junior and senior years have a variety of clinical practice experiences that provide students with a rich diversity of opportunities for service learning. (4) The final element for service learning is reflection. The experience must include the process of reflection about the meaning of the service learning experience. Seminars, post-clinical group discussions, professional diaries, and critical thinking journals are all part of the course expectations in clinical nursing courses. The addition of reflection about the meaning of the service learning experience was all that was needed. Faculty further discussed ways to incorporate the four elements of service learning into each clinical course to help students realize that they were actively engaged in service learning as well as in preparing to become professional nurses.

The following four upper-division nursing courses (Nursing 301, Nursing 302, Nursing 401, and Nursing 402) were selected for inclusion in the service learning expansion goal of the university because they all have community-based components.

NURSING 301: NURSING CARE OF CHILDREN AND THE CHILDBEARING FAMILY

Nursing 301 is designed to help students apply the nursing process in the care of the child and the childbearing family. Emphasis is placed on helping the child and the childbearing family meet their needs through a process of adaptation. Practicum experiences allow the students to assist the child and the childbearing family in adapting to stressors of the environment common to their developmental stage in wellness and illness settings. Historical perspectives and current issues that affect the practice of nursing with the childbearing family and the child are addressed.

The Nursing 301 syllabus provides information about student assignments that are also service learning activities. All students enrolled in Nursing 301 participate in these activities during the semester and gain academic credit for service learning.

Every Touch Counts

The Every Touch Counts program is a service learning activity that was funded by a Nursing 301 faculty grant through the Louisiana Children's Trust Fund. The program was designed to help prevent child abuse by providing pregnant women with appropriate parenting skills. The students prepare and teach the classes, which include preparation for childbirth and child care classes such as nurturing, diapering, bathing, feeding, safety, and discipline. They interact with the participants (pregnant women accompanied by their husbands, boyfriends, mothers, or others), answering questions and awarding door prizes for attendance.

Obesity Health Education Project

Nursing students enrolled in Nursing 301 implemented an obesity program for 12- and 13-year-old children at an area school. The nursing students developed six health education lessons focusing on health behaviors related to weight, which included: aerobic activity, stretching, body fat analysis, self-esteem, and nutrition. The children were taught the principles of the food guide pyramid and how to read food labels, do dietary recalls, and create exercise logs. They learned practical ways to increase their daily exercise and incorporate healthy choices into their diets. The parents of these children were invited to one of the planned educational sessions.

Open Airways for Schools

Open Airways is a comprehensive curriculum adopted by the American Lung Association for school-aged children with asthma. Implementation of the program as a service learning activity was funded by a Nursing 301 faculty instructional grant through the university. The Nursing 301 students used role-play, games, storytelling, artistic expression, and relaxation exercises to facilitate learning with children in grades 4 through 6. Through this program, the nursing students learned about asthma as well as how to interact with school-aged children.

NURSING 302: NURSING CARE OF YOUNG ADULTS

Nursing 302 is designed to help students understand and be accountable for the utilization of the nursing process with young adults. Emphasis is placed on helping young adults and their families to meet their needs through a process of adaptation. Practice is designed to provide experiences with young adults and their families adapting to stressors common to their stage of the life cycle in wellness and illness settings. Historical perspectives and current issues that affect the practice of nursing with young adults are addressed.

The Nursing 302 syllabus provides information about student assignments that are also service learning activities. All students enrolled in Nursing 302 participate in these activities during the semester and gain academic credit for service learning.

Home Health Clinical Experience

The home health clinical rotation for all students in Nursing 302 has been designated a service learning experience. Students visit clients and families in the community, where they assess the client for level of physical functioning, nature of the illness, and the physician's prognosis. Additionally, they evaluate the home environment, identify teaching needs, assess the psychosocial functioning of the patient and family, and determine the adequacy of client and family support systems. Following each home visit, students reflect in writing about the meaning of the experience. They describe their general feelings regarding the home health clinical experience and evaluate the learning opportunities that support their professional education.

NURSING 401: NURSING CARE OF MIDDLE AND OLDER ADULTS

Emphasis in Nursing 401 is on the utilization of the nursing process with middle-aged and older adults. All major concepts (human beings, health, environment, and nursing) are addressed in each unit of the theory component, and strong emphasis is placed on the major concept of nursing (nursing process, accountability, communication, and role) in the clinical component of the course.

The Nursing 401 syllabus provides information about student assignments that are also service learning activities. All students enrolled in Nursing 401 participate in these activities during the semester and gain academic credit for service learning. Since Nursing 401 has one major focus—Medical-Surgical Nursing—the entire clinical component of Nursing 401 is designated as a service learning experience. As such, the experience is based upon the four common elements of service learning: addresses a human need, is experiential in nature, incorporates reciprocity, and incorporates reflection.

NURSING 402: COMPREHENSIVE NURSING

Nursing 402 is designed to help students to utilize the nursing process in acute care and community settings and to analyze and synthesize the nursing needs of clients and their families. Practicums are designed to provide experiences in which students are accountable for designing and implementing nursing care plans to assist in adapting to stressors of environment in illness and wellness settings in varied stages of the life cycle. Leadership/management principles emphasizing professional role development in relation to nursing practice and case management will be utilized in practicum experiences in a variety of settings. Current and future approaches to comprehensive nursing care with clients will be addressed.

The Nursing 402 syllabus provides information about student assignments that are also service learning activities. All students enrolled in Nursing 402 participate in these activities during the semester and gain academic credit for service learning. Service learning experiences are evident throughout the syllabus.

Village du Lac

This is an independent-living housing complex for mentally and physically handicapped individuals who require government assistance to meet their housing needs. Nursing 402 students hold a biweekly health promotion clinic with the residents in this setting, where they provide individualized health screening and counseling. The residents are given health-related information and are assisted in setting short-term, attainable health promotion goals. Students also provide referrals and complete follow-up phone calls and goal achievement evaluations.

Evangeline Health Promotion Program

This is another health promotion program that is held by Nursing 402 students and faculty for residents of the historic Evangeline Hotel. The building provides living space for older adults who require government assistance to meet their housing needs. The residents receive health screening, health counseling, health information, and encouragement with goal setting. "**Remember When**" is a weekly reminiscent group activity that is facilitated by faculty and students to encourage socialization and to help build self-esteem among the residents.

The Well

This is a day shelter for the homeless. Nursing students provide weekly health promotion group activities. They also see guests individually for assessment of health-related complaints and treatment of basic first aid wound care needs. Students learn that change is the responsibility of each individual.

St. Joseph Shelter for Men

This is a residential shelter for the homeless who are in need of transitional housing. Nursing 402 students hold a weekly health promotion clinic at the shelter, where they work with the residents and offer many health education programs that include topics such as information about medications, blood pressure control, early cancer detection, and diabetes management. Students also assist in annual flu immunization clinics and provide continuing health education about basic wound care, first aid, CPR, the Heimlich maneuver, and management of seizures and diabetic emergencies for shelter staff and volunteers.

Juvenile Detention Home

Juveniles who have committed a federal crime are placed in custody in this home, where they are able to continue their formal education. These juveniles are at high risk in our society, and nursing students become aware of the diverse needs of this group. Nursing 402 students present health promotion projects as part of the school day on a weekly basis. Health education activities address exercise, nutrition, hygiene, sexually transmitted diseases, blood-borne pathogens, substance abuse, stress, moods, emotions, anger, and conflict resolution. Nursing students are excellent role models for these juveniles and provide individual counseling, guidance, and support with school assignments, problems, and career choices.

Faith House
This house provides temporary shelter for women and children who are victims of domestic violence. Nursing 402 students provide weekly health promotion programs on topics that address the physical, emotional, financial, and social needs of this particular group. Topics include stress reduction, parenting issues, childhood diseases and disease prevention, nutrition and hygiene, exercise and relaxation, self-defense, and financial assistance. Nursing students also hold health assessment clinics at Faith House, where they conduct hearing testing, vision screening, and screening for diabetes and heart disease.

Health Promotion Home Visiting Program
Each student in Nursing 402 is assigned to an older adult household and makes at least six home visits during the semester. Most of the clients are older adults with chronic health problems. The focus of the visits is health promotion through individualized health screening, health counseling and teaching, short-term goal setting, referral to community services, and follow-up phone calls and/or visits. Students become aware of life changes that must be adapted to by older adults who wish to remain independent in their own homes.

Community-As-A-Client
The purpose of this project is to assess the strengths and needs of a community in relation to physical and mental health. Each clinical group of six students selects a community as a client for the semester. The students in each group share their findings and recommendations with community leaders. This experience helps students to realize that individuals and families exist within communities and that responsibility for community well-being is a shared outcome.

Incorporation of service learning into the nursing curriculum has resulted in numerous benefits for the students, the faculty, the university, the clients, and the community. Students have been overwhelmingly positive about the experiences. Service learning has provided enrichment opportunities that were not possible in the classroom. Experiential learning and collaborative efforts that address community needs have promoted learning and have increased feelings of social responsibility. As a result of the service learning experiences within the nursing curriculum, students have continued to be actively involved in the needs of society. For example, one student discovered that his patient was going home in a wheelchair and the home was not wheelchair accessible. This student enlisted his fraternity brothers' help, and they built a wheelchair ramp one weekend. Another student organized a blood drive for an individual in the community. Other students offer services at the various shelters and community-based walk-in clinics. Students have become involved with activities such as rural school safety projects, health promotion projects across the life span, and working with the Girl Scouts. Faculty have experienced increased opportunities for professional development through grant writing, research, publications, and professional presentations about service learning. Student enthusiasm for the service learning projects has been rewarding for faculty. The College of Nursing has supported its mission through service learning, has received recognition and praise for integrating service learning into the curriculum, and serves as a role model for other university disciplines. The experiences of faculty and students with service learning in the nursing curriculum are shared regularly with the university Service Leaning Council and are disseminated across campus. The university has been able to support its mission and has received recognition for promoting partnerships and collaborative efforts between education and community. The community has received significant help in identifying and meeting the physical, emotional, safety, health, and social needs of its members. The development of partnerships has paved the way for ongoing collaborative endeavors. The community has demonstrated appreciation by donating funds for endowed chairs and professorships for faculty. The reciprocal benefits that occur with the incorporation of service learning into a university curriculum provide the foundation for creative and innovative ways to promote quality of life with limited resources.

REFERENCES

Jacoby, B. (1996). *Service-learning in higher education: Concepts and Practices*. San Francisco: Jossey-Bass.

TEACHING UNDERGRADUATE RESEARCH AND GROUP LEADERSHIP SKILLS THROUGH SERVICE LEARNING PROJECTS

Dr. Marjorie A. Schaffer
Dr. Sandra J. Peterson

In the mid 1990s, several factors contributed to the choice to introduce service learning as a teaching methodology into our senior-level theory course that focused on developing nursing research and leadership skills. We were dissatisfied with student learning about research and our methods of teaching research skills. Generating student enthusiasm for nursing research seemed to be an unrealistic outcome. Our institutional mission strongly emphasized commitment to service as a graduate outcome. In addition, faculty development opportunities provided a foundation in the principles of service learning and funds for integrating service learning into existing courses. In 1996, we instituted service learning into the senior-level course, have evaluated student and community partner experiences several times since then, and have learned how to more fully integrate service learning principles into the curriculum.

PRINCIPLES OF SERVICE LEARNING

Through involvement in faculty development activities and evaluations of the service learning experiences, we identified six principles as most essential to the promotion of successful service learning experiences. The faculty development activities included attendance at both local and national conferences and participation in on-campus discussion groups. Evaluation of the service learning experiences was completed by students through surveys and focus groups, by community partners through telephone interviews, and by faculty during team meetings. These data emphasized the importance of the following principles: (a) students are engaged in useful service as defined by the community partner; (b) the service is clearly related to course objectives; (c) adequate attention is paid to the preparation of both students and the community partner for the service learning experience; (d) mechanisms for meaningful reflection are clearly identified for students; (e) faculty members are involved with both students and the community partner throughout the experience; and (f) ideally the students, community partner, and faculty member together engage in evaluation of the experience.

SERVICE LEARNING: EARLY LESSONS

The curricular application of service learning presented here has evolved over five years of experience in collaboration with a variety of community partners. Initially, a team of four faculty members taught the course. Although all instructors did not fully support the service learning concept, all agreed to a project format for student work. In the first year, service learning projects were piloted in five of eight student groups. Subsequent student feedback revealed that students viewed service-oriented projects as meaningful work that increased their enthusiasm for learning.

Evaluation of student learning and community partner perspectives has contributed to (a) increased integration of service learning concepts into course content and assignments and (b) development of guidelines for developing academic-community partnerships for undergraduate research (Peterson & Schaffer, 1999; Schaffer & Peterson, 1998). For example, early feedback regarding the lack of clarity on the concept of service learning and confusion about students' role and work in community agencies led to adding an introductory class on service learning. In collaboration with community partners, we initiated a structured student orientation to the community agencies with clarification of expectations for student work. Community partners expressed that projects seemed to end abruptly and asked for more interactions with students about their learning. Consequently, an evaluation component on project effectiveness was added to course requirements.

SERVICE LEARNING: APPLIED LESSONS

Service learning is the organizing framework in the course design of a four-credit, semester-long course that includes content on research, leadership, and professional issues. Other than exams, all assignments are related to service learning projects. Students specify their top three choices among six to eight projects that involve implementing a component of the research process. The teaching team selects group membership based on student preference and distribution of student characteristics. Course faculty members collaborate with community partners to identify the need for the research-related activity. Often community partners are agencies that may not have access to time or resources for needed research activities. Student activities provide both a needed service to the community partner and real-world learning experiences that meet the course objectives for students (Weigert, 1998).

Seven to eight students work as a team to implement the project. The faculty member provides orientation, ongoing consultation, and collaboration with the community partner to ensure project quality and completion (with a maximum of three groups per instructor). At the beginning of the course, students, the community partner, and the instructor sign a contract specifying the project activities and time commitment. Instructors monitor progress and provide students with suggestions for implementing the research process. Each student is expected to contribute 10 to 15 hours of direct service; the project groups have an additional 6 hours of class time throughout the semester for group planning and activities.

Assessment of student learning focuses on project management, research, group participation, and reflection on the meaning of service and growth in leadership. Both individual and group assignments are required. Project management assignments are all group assignments and include (a) a project plan with project goal(s), objectives, action steps, and criteria for success; (b) minutes of four of the group meetings; and (c) evaluation of project effectiveness, which can be done in a written format or orally with all group members present. Community partners are invited to the group discussion about project effectiveness and student learning. Students are asked to evaluate the project using the following categories: goal achievement, organization and timeliness, responses to problems, strengths and weaknesses of the project, recommendations for needed changes, and overall satisfaction.

All students identify an individual research question and complete a literature review on a topic related to their service learning project. The project groups write a group paper based on the research process. In addition, each group presents its research-based service learning project in both formal written and oral presentation formats. Community partners often attend the presentations.

Since a major emphasis of the course is learning how to work in a team, students are asked to evaluate the participation of all group members. Each student completes an evaluation form that addresses the contributions of other team members. The evaluation components, ranked on a four-point scale, include participation, resource sharing, interdependence, esteem building, self-expression, listening, showing of respect for self and others, possibility thinking, goal-setting, and conflict management.

Each group of students can select the point value they wish to assign to group participation, the group paper, and the group presentation by distributing 50 of the course points (20% of total points) to these assignments. Many student groups choose to give greater value to group participation, which becomes a motivator for contributing to the work of the group.

With our growing awareness of the importance of reflection as a key principle of effective service learning (Eyler & Giles, Jr., 1999; Jacoby, 1996), we have modified assignments to encourage critical thinking about the meaning of the students' experience in service learning. In a paper, students are asked to reflect on their definition of service or their relationship with the community partner. A second paper on leadership and teamwork encourages students to reflect on growth in leadership by peers and self, effective and ineffective teamwork practices, and advice for promoting leadership development in the newly practicing nurse.

In order to provide students with opportunity to reflect on their experiences as a group and to provide closure to the course, we have added an action-oriented group reflection assignment. Student groups enact the meaning of their service learning experiences. For example, one group is asked to create a giant Likert scale (Eyler, Giles Jr., & Schmiede, 1996). This student group writes several items about satisfaction with their learning and then asks class members to move to one of five stations in the room representing a point on the Likert scale, from strongly agree to strongly disagree. Another student group creates a group sculpture (using their bodies to form the sculpture) for the words *teamwork, leadership,* and *service.* The students then ask their classmates to interpret each of the group sculptures. Examples of other group reflection exercises include role-playing a work group meeting (effective and ineffective); role-playing a television news spot about service learning at the college; and composing a song, rap, poem, or cheer about their service learning experience.

PLANNING FOR SERVICE LEARNING PROJECTS

During the first year of implementing service learning projects, we learned that careful preparation and collaboration with community partners prior to student contact was essential to effectively using service learning as a teaching methodology. For a spring semester course, we begin to identify potential service learning partnerships early in the fall with the goal of establishing an agreement by the end of the semester. A key principle underlying the agreement is to give control of identification of the service to the community partner (Sigmon, 1979). We ask community partners to suggest a research-related need that students can meet by working in a team. In the month prior to the first class, instructors meet with community partners to identify the specific project focus and to plan student orientation. Written project descriptions and a schedule of initial meetings are available for students on the first day of class. After initial meetings and orientation with students and community partners, instructors divide their consultation time among three groups during the scheduled class work groups.

ONGOING MANAGEMENT OF SERVICE LEARNING PROJECTS

Although service learning projects may be well planned with optimal community input and student orientation, we have discovered the need to be prepared to respond to the unexpected and unplanned. We have experienced the challenge of making wise decisions about the timing and degree of intervention to provide when students and community partners experience frustration, dissatisfaction, or failure. Some of the sources of dissatisfaction we have encountered include (a) failure of the reality of the situation to match expectations, (b) conflicts between community partners' needs for service delivery and students' academic schedules, (c) students' perceptions of inequality of investment of time between and within groups, and (d) a differing sense of urgency about the need for communication and decision making between community partner, students, and faculty member. If we determine it is appropriate to intervene, the process usually involves renegotiation of expectations. We have also discovered that it is important for the faculty member to communicate a sense of passion and commitment to the project in order for students to maintain their belief in the importance of what they are doing.

SERVICE LEARNING PROJECT EXAMPLES

We have collaborated with a variety of community partners, including state and local government agencies, many private nonprofit agencies, a few hospitals, and numerous churches. In partnership with state and local government agencies, students have collected data on immunization rates among children under two years of age, have reviewed Community Health Service Plans for mental health strategies, and have collected data on the working order of smoke detectors in homes in a high-risk neighborhood.

Private nonprofit organizations have included a block nurse program for the elderly, an after-school program, a shelter for victims of family violence, clinics serving low-income neighborhoods, a crisis nursery, and an agency that provided a furniture warehouse for low-income families. Student activities have involved conducting focus groups and surveys on health care needs, conducting a survey on employee smoking habits, and offering a health promotion event. One service learning project took place in a long-term care facility, and two were in hospitals. In one of these, student research activities were integrated into an existing study on asthma and allergies.

Nursing faculty members' interest in parish nursing has resulted in numerous partnerships with local churches, often in collaboration with a parish nurse. In many partnerships with churches, students have completed a health needs assessment of the congregation and have developed recommendations for health-related programs for the congregation. Other projects have involved health promotion education and a community blood drive. When data collection is not the primary activity of the project, students use qualitative or quantitative data analysis to determine the effectiveness of the intervention.

The following examples describe in more detail four of the nearly thirty projects that we have implemented. These examples demonstrate our efforts to integrate the principles of service learning.

Health Needs Assessment of a Homeless Population

The Nursing Department and an agency that provided health care to a homeless population had a history of collaborating on student clinical placements. The agency director suggested that a survey of the health needs of clients served in the clinics would be useful to the agency. The survey form, developed by the faculty member and the agency director, was reviewed by clinic staff and was piloted with homeless clients seeking health care services. In an orientation provided during class at the college, the agency director described clinic sites and explained processes for contacting staff and clients. The faculty member provided protocol for the research process. Students collected survey data from 101 homeless individuals at three shelters with clinics. In addition, the agency director and one student conducted a focus group with ten women at a shelter for homeless families. Student and community partner concerns that were resolved during the project included student communication with clinic staff about the timing and process of data collection, conflicts with schedules, decision making about feasible strategies for obtaining the targeted number of surveys, and strategies for data analysis.

The agency identified several modifications for provision of care based on qualitative and quantitative data from the surveys. Identified needs included convenient access to dental care, chiropractic services, self-care and prevention-oriented education, promotion of healthy eating patterns at shelters, education about use of health care services and emergency care, and integration of spirituality into health care delivery. Following completion of the project, the community partner recommended that the orientation of the students should occur in the setting where services are provided rather than at the college. Also, the community partner commented that student learning would have been enhanced by additional time to reflect on their understanding of the experience of homelessness. The outcomes of this partnership were featured in two publications authored by the faculty member, the agency director, and a senior student (Gustafson, Mather, & Schaffer, 1999; Schaffer, Mather, & Gustafson, in press).

Review of Community Health Service Plans

One faculty member had collaborated with staff from the Minnesota Health Department (MDH) on several small research studies, which provided familiarity with current MDH initiatives. When asked about possible data-collection projects that might be useful to MDH as well as feasible for senior nursing students, the suicide-prevention coordinator suggested the identification of mental health needs and strategies found in the Community Health Service (CHS) Plans. The student group reviewed 50 CHS plans submitted by community health boards to determine community needs and priorities regarding suicide and mental health. This project was described in the *Report to the Minnesota Legislature: Suicide Prevention Plan* as a component of the MDH 2000 Action Plan (Minnesota Health Department, 2000). The MDH suicide-prevention coordinator and school mental health coordinator created a tool consisting of key questions for guiding the review of CHS plans. They provided an orientation at an MDH location that included a description of the organization of community health boards in the state, the content of CHS plans, the review tool, and logistics in accessing the CHS plans. Students divided the 50 CHS plans among group members and completed the review tool electronically. The community partner read the initial plan reviews completed by students and suggested modifications for streamlining the process to reduce the amount of time students were investing in completing the reviews.

Once students completed the CHS plans reviews, the data were sent electronically to the community partner. Midway through the semester, community partners met with the students to guide their data interpretation phase of the project. Since the review tool included a large amount of data, it was decided that the students would complete the portion that would be most beneficial to the community partner. One problem encountered by the group was the variability in the completeness of reviews among students in the group. When analyzing the data, students determined that some plans had been less thoroughly reviewed. The group members needed to decide how to handle the data in a way that would accurately report conclusions about the CHS plans and work through dissatisfaction with inequality in student performance among group members.

Late in the semester, the community partners met with the faculty member and student group to discuss the results and to evaluate the effectiveness of the project. Based on the data, students recommended that the health department provide assistance to local community health agencies on (a) assessment strategies for identifying community health needs, (b) educational strategies for increasing public awareness on the importance of mental health for community well-being, and (c) development of clear problem statements and specific, time-oriented criteria for evaluation related to mental health in the CHS plans. The community partners, who expressed great satisfaction with the work and conclusions of the student group, stated that the data would provide support for decision making on the response to mental health needs in the state. Although students indicated that the time investment was excessive, they also expressed satisfaction in the completion of a meaningful project in which the data were useful for decision making about the state's response to mental health needs.

Survey on Depression and Medication Use

The administrative staff of a skilled long-term care facility became concerned about the number of residents for whom antidepressant medications were being prescribed. This facility's rate of prescription exceeded the state average. The director of nurses wanted additional information about this finding. To plan for student involvement, the faculty member met several times with the director of nurses and the facility's consulting pharmacologist to identify research questions, to develop methodology, and to determine processes that were needed in both the agency and the college to proceed with the study. In this research project, the students were responsible for the collection of data. To prepare them for this responsibility, the director of nurses, a social worker, and the faculty member conducted an orientation and training session at the facility. During this session, students were introduced to the survey instrument developed by the faculty member, examined a sample chart, and were instructed on the administration of the Geriatric Depression Scale.

For those residents who gave consent, students were randomly assigned to complete a chart review and to administer the depression scale. During the data collection, the faculty member addressed two problems. Students found unit staff uninformed about the project, and students complained about the quality and quantity of the work of other group members. To address the problem of uninformed staff, the faculty member contacted the director of nurses who provided the necessary information to the staff. To address the problem of group member involvement, the faculty member encouraged the students to attempt to work through their concerns as a group. The students did devote one of their group work sessions to a discussion of their interactional problems. The students summarized the collected data using descriptive statistics and presented these findings to facility personnel. The consulting pharmacologist was responsible for conducting further data analysis on the relationships between the incidence of depression determined by the depression scale, the behavioral indicators of depression as found in the charts, and the use of antidepressant medications.

Health Needs of the Elderly

The faculty member contacted the parish nurse of a large suburban church. With only a part-time position and a congregation of over 8,000 members, it was not difficult for the parish nurse to identify a need that students could be involved in meeting. The elderly population of the congregation frequently sought her services for a variety of health care issues. To better serve this population, the nurse wished to have a clearer understanding of the major health concerns of the homebound elderly and the community resources available to address those needs. In addition, she wanted a booklet describing relevant health care resources that she could distribute to parishioners. Prior to the involvement of students, the faculty member revised an already existing health needs assessment instrument, and the parish nurse arranged an orientation program and identified homebound elderly who were willing to be interviewed. As part of their orientation to this project, students accompanied one of the pastors on a home visit.

The student-conducted home visits and interviews proceeded without complication. Though other needs emerged during the analysis of the data, transportation was the one most frequently expressed. The students renegotiated the second phase of the project, the development of a booklet of relevant resources. Because the students found an agency that provided referrals for a wide range of care services for the elderly, they provided the parish nurse with information about this agency instead of developing the booklet. This parish nurse has continued to be involved in service learning projects.

BENEFITS OF SERVICE LEARNING

From evaluation data, we have identified numerous benefits for students, community partners, and faculty. Students identified fewer benefits during the service learning experience than they did after its completion. Community partners emphasized the direct contribution to the work of their agencies as a benefit (Peterson & Schaffer, 1999; Schaffer & Peterson, 1998). Faculty experienced greater satisfaction through increased student engagement in learning.

The benefit most consistently identified by students was the development of leadership skills. They commented on developing increased comfort with the role of group leader, learning how to motivate others and resolve conflict, recognizing the inevitability of change, and becoming more flexible when the unexpected occurs. Students also reflected on how much a team accomplished when each member assumed ownership of the project and recognized the strengths and contributions of others. After completing service learning projects, students identified the additional benefit of learning about the research process. They expressed that research "came to life," was useful for nursing practice, and contributed to an inquiry-oriented way of thinking.

For community partners and faculty members, benefits more often come with some risk. Ideally, for community partners, service learning projects will result in data that can contribute to the accomplishment of a goal that they had identified. One of the risks that community partners may experience is the investment of time with no assurance of the quality of the data. Also, an additional expenditure of time and energy may be required when relating to students who are encountering a system that they do not fully understand.

As faculty members, we have been gratified by students' increased interest in nursing research and its significance to practice. Students have demonstrated a higher level of commitment to their learning experiences and an excitement about being engaged in what they perceive to be meaningful work. The risks experienced by faculty members are similar to those of the community partner. These risks include a significant investment of time and energy in establishing and maintaining community partner relationships and relating to students who are uncomfortable with uncertainty or dissatisfied with the project process.

CONCLUSION

We believe the benefits in learning for students about the research process, leadership skills, and teamwork and the benefit of service to the community partner outweigh expressions of dissatisfaction about group process and time investment during the project. Once students have completed the group project, they express satisfaction in the accomplishment of meaningful work and their development of leadership skills. Indeed, working through the problems encountered in meaningful service learning projects can equip students with skills they need for interacting in a demanding and challenging health care world. To conclude, the following words of a graduate provide evidence for the potential of service learning:

> I think [in] so many of the experiences I had as a nursing student, I didn't really feel like I was partnering with the people I was working with in clinicals and the hospitals. They were making room for me to be there but I didn't really feel like I was partnering with them. Whereas, in this research I felt I was collaborating with the people that I was working with. And that was a really empowering experience for me.

REFERENCES

Eyler, J., & Giles, Jr., D. E. (1999). *Where's the learning in service-learning?* San Francisco: Jossey-Bass.

Eyler, J., Giles Jr., D. E., & Schmiede, A. (1996). *A practitioner's guide to reflection in service learning.* Nashville, TN: Vanderbilt University.

Gustafson, V., Mather, S., & Schaffer, M. A. (1999). Who is my neighbor?: Reflections on serving the homeless. *Journal of Christian Nursing,* 16(1), 12–15.

Jacoby, B. (1996). *Service learning in higher education: Concepts and practices.* San Francisco: Jossey-Bass.

Minnesota Health Department. (2000, January 15). *Report to the Minnesota legislature: Suicide prevention plan.* St. Paul, MN: Minnesota Health Department, Family Health Division.

Peterson, S. J., & Schaffer, M. (1999). Service learning: A strategy to develop group collaboration and research skills. *Journal of Nursing Education,* 38(5), 208–214.

Schaffer, M. A., Mather, S., & Gustafson, V. (in press). Service learning: A strategy for conducting a health needs assessment of the homeless. *Journal of Health Care for the Poor and Underserved.*

Schaffer, M. A., & Peterson, S. J. (1998). Service learning as a strategy for teaching undergraduate research. *The Journal of Experiential Education,* 21(3), 154–161.

Sigmon, R. (1979). Service learning: Three principles. *Synergist,* 8(1), 9–11.

Weigert, K. M. (1998). Academic service learning: Its meaning and relevance. In R. A. Rhoads & J. P. F. Howard (Eds.), *Academic service learning: A pedagogy of action and reflection,* (No. 73, pp. 3–10). San Francisco: Jossey-Bass.

CHAPTER

SERVICE LEARNING WITH VICTIMS OF DOMESTIC VIOLENCE

Dr. Mary B. Neiheisel
Dr. Carolyn Delahoussaye

Nursing is a practice discipline, and inherent in this practice is service. Graduate students are a diverse group of individuals who bring to the graduate situation a wide diversity of professional and personal experiences, a sense of responsibility to the human race, a civic pride, and an obligation to improve society. They are pursuing careers as primary care providers to multiple-risk populations that represent all age groups, reflect a variety of ethnic and cultural backgrounds, and have common and complex health care needs. Clinical experiences for graduate students become service learning through integrated practice in community settings where reciprocal, collaborative, inquiry-based learning occurs and contributions to the community reflect awareness of societal needs.

Frequently, people who are abused suffer physical, emotional, sexual, substance, and/or financial abuse. They may be anyone in our society, including children, spouses of both genders, elderly, or residents of shelters or nursing homes. In this article persons who are abused will be portrayed as the wives and children of men who are abusive and will be designated as victims of domestic violence. Battered women and their traumatized children are a complex problem. The impact of this problem on society has been monumental. As a result of the high percentage of battered women—probably as great as 25%—new laws have been passed that specifically address the mental needs, social services, and legal requirements of this group. The Violence Against Women Act of 1994 included a $1.3 billion appropriation, and states have followed suit in attaching some type of appropriation to the state laws. Documentation has shown that bipolar disorders, depression, anxiety attacks, post-traumatic stress disorder (PTSD), panic disorder, phobias, acute stress disorders, substance abuse, and/or suicidal ideation are prevalent among battered women. Approximately 35% of all emergency department visits are made by victims of abuse. Domestic violence inflicts more injuries on women than accidents, muggings, and cancer deaths combined. In response, numerous crisis shelters have been built, and social, mental, and pharmacological services have been made available to the battered women of America. Multidisciplinary interventions related to the sexual, physical, and psychological trauma experienced by these women have been instituted (Roberts, 1998). The economic impact alone is monumental. It is estimated that the cost per month of maintaining a forty-bed facility is approximately $30,000. This cost includes building maintenance, utilities, cleaning, lawn care, and so on but does not include salaries. The donations of food, clothing, and incidentals probably reduce this cost by $10,000 to $15,000. The average shelter has a mean annual operating budget of about $160,000 for personnel, consisting of 6 full-time and four part-time paid staff and 25 volunteers. The residents receive shelter, clothing, food, and counseling, and, in return, they help with the physical maintenance of the facility.

Although the problem of domestic violence in our society is prevalent, illegal, and mind-shattering, denial of its existence has been prominent. Battered women perpetuate this denial due to embarrassment, terror, and/or fear of reprisal. Prior to 1940, victims of domestic violence received shelter, personal assistance, court advocacy, equitable property settlements, and protection only through divorce. In the late 1940s, protective services were replaced by crime prevention services, and assistance to battered women was neglected until the feminist movement of the 1970s. The proof of this denial is evidenced by the fact that there were no articles published on domestic violence from 1939 to 1969 in *The Journal of Marriage and Family Therapy,* only 30 articles published from 1969 to 1986, and no significant increase noted since 1986 (Roberts, 1998).

The absence of research and literature related to domestic violence has created a void in the educational preparation of graduate nursing students. Therefore, a domestic violence shelter that provides temporary housing and protection for battered women and their children was selected as a clinical site so that students would gain first-hand information about victims of domestic violence, the prominence of domestic violence in our society, and some of the health care needs of the shelter residents. This shelter has been in existence for 15 years, but in-house health care has been available only during the past year for approximately eight hours per week.

As care moves from hospital to community settings, preparations need to be made for health and wellness promotion roles with vulnerable populations. Health promotion in vulnerable populations is crucial, and battered women are a vulnerable group. Health care providers have greater opportunities than ever for working with and for these clients in an optimum service learning setting. The health care provider and the client are both responsible, but the health care provider, with knowledge of health promotion and resources, has the greater burden.

One of the objectives of the clinical course is health promotion. The first step in health promotion is assessment, followed by collaborative goal setting. Health promotion for battered women involves women from all cultures and all socioeconomic groups across the life span and begins with three steps: providing information, facilitating self-assessment, and goal setting. Health promotion includes screening for evidence of abuse and questioning the client concerning her knowledge about the following: (1) is she in danger? (2) are there lethal weapons in the home? (3) does she have a safe escape route and destination? The woman should be given immediate information that will enable her to get protection for herself and her loved ones.

In abusive situations health is commonly neglected, and the battered woman may feel that this neglect can continue until she takes care of other priorities. It is necessary to work with the client to develop a comfortable plan in which priorities and health promotion measures are addressed. The health assessment tools to be used with this vulnerable population include a complete health history, health promotion practices, and assessment of knowledge of and/or exposure to sexually transmitted diseases. Since the abused woman will be living in a community-type setting, she needs to be given requirements for cleanliness, hygiene, and prevention of the spread of respiratory infections and other communicable diseases. Based on the information from the self-assessment guides, goals will be established with the client and a plan for meeting these goals will be developed.

Faculty members believe that clinical experiences for graduate students in a domestic violence shelter should be professional, experiential service learning practice. Outcome goals for the students include learning the signs of abuse and the appropriate empathetic responses, identifying resources for the victims, building communication skills to be used in crisis situations, specifying appropriate interventions, and refining critical thinking skills. In addition, the authors believe that a well-rounded educational program assists students to understand the totality of society, the characteristics of their community, the completeness of education, and the whole of contributions to society. Service learning contributes to community service and insures a more complete education by involving students in community service projects. Service learning is frequently singled out as an entity in itself, whereas, in truth, it should be a part of the whole. Service to learn is an integrated part of the whole of nursing. The clinical experiences of student nurses are primarily activities with populations in community agencies such as hospitals, school-based clinics, and home health agencies. Students who practice in the domestic violence shelter interact with and counsel residents who have experienced and express real fear and the loss of power, self-respect, and self-esteem. The graduate nursing students were scheduled to provide the following services: blood pressure monitoring; vision, hearing, and depression screening; health history and physical assessments; interventions for minor problems and injuries; and counseling.

The orientation to life at the shelter and to domestic violence included cold, dark facts from an experienced, knowledgeable person who is the director of the facility. Life experiences, readings, and multimedia releases had all contributed to the students' knowledge and feelings about domestic violence. Actually being in the facility and talking to the director introduced them to a reality never before experienced. As they toured the area, they met women and children who simply reached out for a touch, a hug, attention, and confirmation of a belief that someone cared. As the students began their history taking and physical examinations, they heard stories about all types of abuse—physical, verbal, economic, emotional, and sexual. They learned about the hatred and meanness that occurs before and after the wife finally leaves. The phrases "lowered self-esteem" and "starting over" were redefined for the students by the actions of the victims they met. As the students increased their skills in listening to heart and breath sounds, examining eyes and ears, and multiple other skills, the residents found a listening ear, an empathetic person, and a person who also helped them with physical problems.

Graduate nursing students have been taught how to carry out crisis intervention and have gained information about what to do and where to go. The actual encounter with victims of domestic violence through a clinical experience at the shelter is a profound learning experience for students. Seeing injuries, lowered self-esteem, and powerlessness; hearing the reiteration of the abuse; reading court protective custody and restraining orders; and watching a mom looking through donated clothing for herself and her children provide a framework for health care that can only be obtained from the victims. The active learning helped to demonstrate the relevance and importance of the academic classroom and clinical materials.

One of the course objectives is to identify risk factors. The students assessed a number of clients with asthma and/or major smoking problems and volunteered to administer influenza vaccinations. Upon learning that tuberculosis testing was scheduled by the Health Care Advocate, they volunteered to assist with these activities. Tuberculosis testing is required, but the influenza vaccine was done with informed consent. This experience involved the community and necessitated locating donors of the materials needed for tuberculosis testing and influenza vaccinations. Again, the students participated in an endeavor to improve the health of individuals, which in turn improved the health of the community. Health information topics identified by the students were parenting skills, over-the-counter medications, breast self-examination, nutrition, nicotine addiction, depression, and when to call the nurse practitioner.

The residents were able to convey their personal, daily life needs with objectivity, and as a result, students reflected pride in their community for maintaining this facility. The students were able to give beneficial health care to the residents. In addition, all students made donations of incidentals and over-the-counter medications that are used by the residents. An excellent example of humanness and caring is the student who volunteered to care for two dogs for a resident and her children. The student had read an article about pet therapy and then witnessed a resident who took only her children, her dogs, and a few clothes when she left her husband and her home. Although the shelter provides facilities for the residents, the only option for the dogs was to have the resident take them to the pound. The student, who had the space as well as children to love the dogs, took care of them for over two months. He was able to empathize with the resident's pain of parting with her family pets. The faculty member believes that the student felt more of a sense of "this is life" rather than the global concept of "a giving back" for a better community. Over time and with multiple similar incidents, the student will, no doubt, interpret such actions as civic participation and a type of partnership with the resident of this facility.

The coping mechanisms learned and the solutions identified within this student learning experience will assist the student as he/she enters the primary care provider role and career, which will involve multiple societal problems. For example, the health care provider's clientele will include all types of abuse that are characterized by dependency, innocence, defenselessness, exposure, helplessness, naivete, powerlessness, and susceptibility. Nurses view the susceptible as those being most likely to develop a physical, mental, emotional, or psychological disability, or the group more likely to experience physical, mental, emotional, sexual, and/or pharmacological abuse. Stanhope and Knollmueller (1997) conceptualize vulnerability as multidimensional and depict these dimensions in a figure of dynamic interactions, which include limited control, victimization, disadvantaged status, disenfranchisement, powerlessness, and health risks. Perhaps other dimensions that could be added are separateness, isolation, nonsupportiveness, and resourcelessness. The students identified many of these dimensions and viewed with increased understanding some of the societal issues. They reflected upon their experiences through journaling and recorded an increased desire to investigate other shelters in the area, to volunteer time with the underserved, and to provide more services to the shelter as well as other facilities in the area. The interest and energy expressed by the students led to a collaboration among the University Communicative Disorders faculty and students and the graduate nursing students to conduct hearing tests for the children, the women, and the staff of the shelter. This activity contributed to an interdisciplinary and an intradisciplinary partnership. Sixty percent of the graduate students volunteered, and one hundred percent participated. The benefits of this experience were reciprocal. Two percent of the adult women learned that they needed further testing, and five percent discovered that the learning problems of their children might be due to a hearing problem. The students acquired information about this hearing screening referral resource, and they also increased their skills in testing hearing.

Domestic violence knows no economic, cultural, racial, or ethnic boundaries. Students assess and interact with the residents of the shelter in their rooms, which are shared by women and children of various ages, races, cultures, religions, and economic backgrounds. Available health care resources are minimal, and students use problem solving and critical thinking to alleviate the concerns of the residents. They learn to use every teachable moment to provide health information because contact with the resident is short-term and opportunities for follow-up are minimal. These interactions improve their interpersonal skills, which are so important in achieving success in professional and personal spheres. In addition, the students are exposed to other available resources in the community. The residents and the staff provide the students with information about obtaining food stamps, protective custody orders, temporary restraining orders, the legal system, the public health department, Kid Med, and the medical treatment center for the uninsured, jobless, and poor population.

The health care services actually rendered by the students included recording health histories; completing physical assessments; blood pressure monitoring; vision, depression, and hearing screening; treatment of minor illnesses and injuries; tuberculosis testing; and influenza vaccinations. Students were able to provide these services and analyze the results. A plan was formulated that included treatment, feedback for clients, and teaching and anticipatory guidance related to identified health care needs. The clients provided information to the students about the availability of health care and the health care delivery system in their circumstances.

Reviewing the health histories with the residents enabled the students to practice interview techniques and to explain to the residents the relationship of their family history to their own health and to potential illnesses. The health histories and physical assessments were recorded in formal, organized format. The information was analyzed, a diagnosis was made, and a plan was developed. The plan included health and safety information as well as anticipatory guidance. The plan was discussed with the client, and necessary modifications were made. The residents requested and complied with blood pressure monitoring but were unwilling to make changes such as salt and weight reduction, smoking cessation, and starting exercise programs.

The students prepared eighth-grade-level handouts and distributed them at their classes. The following classes were offered and were followed by evaluations:

1. Nutrition: Residents actively participated with questions and then suggestions to the shelter staff about food purchases and preparation. They discussed changes they planned to make in their diets.
2. Parenting Skills: This was one of the best classes for verbalization and participation. Numerous concerns were related about children and stepchildren and the mother versus the stepmother. Interactive sharing of successes and failures with parenting situations occurred.
3. Breast self-examination: The residents were very interested in this topic and questioned the presenters about correct techniques and breast cancer. Student demonstrations and resident return

demonstrations allowed opportunities for private consultation and critiquing of residents' techniques. The residents were given an additional visual aid, the Breast Self Examination card, which they could place in the area in which they would be completing their self-examination.

4. Over-the-Counter Medications: These residents rely on over-the-counter medications and purchase them indiscriminately without reading labels. Active responses included surprise and appreciation for information that labels should be read in their entirety.

5. When to Seek Health Care Assistance: This was not a popular class and had low reciprocal exchange perhaps because this group has a history of taking their children to a health care facility when they have reached the limits of what they alone can handle.

6. Depression and Bipolar Disorders: This class was requested by the shelter staff and contributed to their knowledge about these conditions and their treatments. The handouts were excellent and indicated outstanding preparation by the student. The feedback proved that essential information is readily received and appreciated. The class actually helped to support the mission of both the university and the facility and created an opportunity to share and to gain recognition for the student and the graduate program.

Teachable, spontaneous moments enabled students to more readily provide crucial information because they occurred in response to an immediate recognized need. For example, several mothers were uninformed that Pepto-Bismol contains salicylates (which are prohibited in children, even though the label lists the safe dose for children) and requested the medicine for their children. They did know about the dangers of aspirin and the relation to Reye's disease. Another safety concern addressed by the students was the bottles of "baby aspirin" in the medication cabinet at the shelter. They learned that these had been purchased for a 59-year-old resident who had a heart condition. The suggested safety measure of removing the aspirin bottles prior to an accidental administration to a child was followed by removal. Following this experience the students began to explore their ethical and moral responsibilities through reflections in their clinical journals. They expressed ways to alert the nation and society about the misnomer of bottles that are labeled "baby aspirin."

The collaborative partnership with the community-based domestic violence shelter fulfilled the four elements of a true service learning experience. The first element mandates that the activity meet a human need and/or solve a community problem. Rising health care costs and decreased availability and accessibility to health care have caused a universal need for improved health promotion, and underserved populations who reside in shelters are a prime example of this deficit. Solving a community problem of this significance is a long-term project; however, the students were able to partially meet the health care and health promotion needs of the shelter residents. As an outcome of this experience, the students became more cognizant of domestic violence and the subsequent problems as well as the efforts of the community to seek solutions.

The second service learning element is an experiential component in which the students applied theory to practice, and in that clinical experience they improved their physical, interpersonal, and critical thinking skills. In the experiences of the nurse practitioner, student learning occurred in relation to seeing people who tolerate violence, who are unsafe, who are powerless, and who have little or no self-esteem or self-respect. Students also learned experientially about the physical, emotional, and cognitive development of children who are the innocent pawns in domestic violence situations.

The third service learning element involves reciprocity toward the community members involved in the service learning experience. The residents are receiving health promotion, health information, emotional counseling, and support. Their health problems are being diagnosed and treated, and as a result, they are experiencing a sense of worth and a sense that someone cares about them and is willing to listen to them. The students learned about the human meaning of poverty; shelter living; cooperative sharing with strangers from diverse cultural and economic backgrounds; dependency upon others for safety, food, clothing, and shelter; and survival measures for homeless abused victims. The reciprocal learning that the students experienced also included a heightened awareness of the value of their own lives. They acknowledged that the opportunities to become educated professionals and to find a fulfilling life style are privileges not to be taken for granted.

The final service learning element is reflection, which was accomplished through the students' writing about critical thinking incidents in which they described the happening, the possible choices of action, the course of action taken, and the outcome. They reflected on whether the intervention was appropriate or should have been different and followed this with evaluation and expression of feelings regarding the incident. In the clinical log the students listed their subjective and objective findings, identification of the diagnoses and health care needs, treatment plan, and the information and anticipatory guidance given to the residents. The plan and teaching were evaluated, and the students determined that patients' ability to follow through with prescriptions and treatment were influenced by available money, time, and other resources. The students consulted with the staff for community resources and possible referral of the residents.

The clinical experiences of the students at the shelter for domestic violence were extremely positive. Students were able to meet the course objectives, address human and societal needs, operate in reciprocal learning relationships, collaborate with a university service, and reflect upon the meaning of the experience. This provided them with the opportunity to engage in service learning within the context of a university-based graduate course.

REFERENCES

Roberts, A. (Ed.). (1998). *Battered women and their families.* New York: Springer.

Stanhope, M., & Knollmueller, R. (1997). *Public and community health nurse's consultant.* St. Louis: Mosby.

United States Department of Health and Human Services, Public Health Service. (1991). *Healthy people 2000: National health promotion and disease prevention objectives.* Washington, DC: U.S. Government Printing Office.

A RESOURCE CENTER FOR YOUNG PARENTS-TO-BE

Dr. Anne Broussard

The Resource Center for Young Parents-To-Be is the most recent phase in the evolution of a student teaching project established by the author in fall 1997. The project has been funded by grants from the Louisiana Children's Trust Fund and by the local Woman's Foundation, and an instructional mini-grant from the university. Each first-semester junior, maternal-child nursing clinical group is given the guidance and resources needed to facilitate learning by pregnant women and their support persons in one of six prenatal topic areas. Currently, every student group is assigned once to each of two sites: (1) the local health unit prenatal clinic attended by pregnant women of lower socioeconomic status and (2) a special school designed to meet the needs of pregnant adolescents.

This activity was designed as a service learning experience to encompass four elements (Jacoby and Associates, 1996). First, the experience attempts to meet human need and/or to solve a community problem. Second, the educational requirements include experiential learning. Third, students and faculty adopt a perspective of reciprocity toward those community members involved in the service learning experience. Lastly, students are required to reflect on their experiences by writing in journals, engaging in exercises designed to produce reflective processing, and/or by participating in group discussion about the meaning of their service learning experiences.

MEETING HUMAN NEEDS/SOLVING COMMUNITY PROBLEMS

The human need to be addressed by the teaching project was lack of knowledge among prospective parents about children's needs, development, and care, which is often a factor contributing to a community problem of child abuse and neglect. Child protection investigations in our parish (county) increased 14% from 1990 to 1996 (Louisiana Children's Trust Fund, 1997). Within the eight-parish Acadiana area, most valid child abuse allegations in 1996 were for neglect, followed by physical abuse. Data from this prevention plan indicate that the child at highest risk in Acadiana in 1996 for abuse and neglect was 10 years of age or older, and the most common perpetrator was a female 30 to 39 years old. The next most common perpetrator was a female between the ages of 19 and 29. The most common male perpetrator was between the ages of 30 and 39.

The assumption is that the most common perpetrator, then, was between 20 and 29 years old at the time of her child's birth, and the next most common perpetrator was an adolescent at the time of her child's birth. Males 30 to 39 years of age were in their twenties at the time of their children's births. The target population for the resource center is 13- to 29-year-old pregnant women along with their support persons or partners. It was hoped that the education and support received in the Resource Center for Young Parents-To-Be would constitute a form of primary prevention for this group of prospective parents in our region who are at higher risk for child abuse and neglect and who may benefit from learning parenting skills during pregnancy or early parenthood.

To meet the parents' need for knowledge about children's needs, development, and care, the Every Touch Counts curriculum. It was adapted for use in the resource center. The Every Touch Counts program was designed by Dr. Velma Butler, a Family Resource specialist. It was adapted with the help of a Louisiana Children's Trust Fund grant, was field tested, and was used by the Lafayette Parish LSU Extension Service Home Economists in our area, mostly with pregnant adolescents. Teachers' manuals and booklets for participants are available from the LSU Cooperative Extension Service (Table 1). The content and activities were divided into five topic areas, and a sixth topic area on pregnancy behaviors and fetal development was added (Table 2).

The author worked closely with the director of nursing at the health unit to set six dates during each semester for the students to staff the resource center in conjunction with scheduled prenatal clinics. The health unit nurses were oriented to the resource center and were encouraged to refer their prenatal clinic clients to the center. At the beginning of each semester, colorful posters with details about the center were hung in the clinic waiting and exam rooms and flyers were given to each pregnant woman attending prenatal clinics. Similar arrangements were made with the director of the school for pregnant adolescents, and the girls were oriented to the resource center concept by the author and given flyers. All materials produced for the resource center consistently contained the same logo and/or colors to increase recognition of the program in the community.

The number of participants in the resource center is increasing as the program becomes more well established and as attention spreads by word-of-mouth. In the spring 2000 semester, 116 visits by 61 pregnant women and 26 support persons were recorded over the six dates the center was provided at the health unit.

TABLE 1 Sources of Prenatal Education Materials to Use in a Resource Center.

Name of Source	Address	Web Site Address	Phone
American Academy of Pediatrics	141 Northwest Point Blvd PO Box 747 Elk Grove Village, IL 60009-0747	aap.org	1-800-433-9016
Birth & Life Bookstore	141 Commercial Street NE Salem, OR 97301	1cascade.com	1-800-443-9942
Channing L. Bete Co., Inc.	200 State Road South Deerfield, MA 01373-0200	channing-bete.com	1-800-628-7733
ETR Associates	PO Box 1830 Santa Cruz, CA 95061-1830	etr.org	1-800-321-4407
HEALTH EDCO/Childbirth Graphics	PO Box 21207 Waco, TX 76702-1207	childbirthgraphics.com	1-800-299-3366, ext. 295/287
ICEA Bookmarks	PO Box 20048 Minneapolis, MN 55420-0048		1-800-624-4934
Injoy Videos	1435 Yarmouth, Suite 102-B Boulder, CO 80304	injoyvideos.com	1-800-326-2082
Journeyworks Publishing	PO Box 8466 Santa Cruz, CA 95061-8466	journeyworks.com	1-800-775-1998
La Leche League International	PO Box 4079 Schaumburg, IL 60168-4079	lalecheleague.org	1-847-519-9585 or 7730

TABLE 1 Sources of Prenatal Education Materials to Use in a Resource Center. (Continued)

Name of Source	Address	Web Site Address	Phone
The Lamaze Media Center	Department 3197 Washington, DC 20042-3197	lamaze-childbirth.org	1-800-368-4404
LSU Cooperative Extension Service		agctr.lsu.edu/wwwac	1-504-388-4141
Motherwear	320 Riverside Dr, Ste C Northampton, MA 01062-9910	motherwear.com	1-800-633-0303
Noodle Soup of Weingart Design	46114 Prospect Avenue #421 Cleveland, OH 44103-4314	noodlesoup.com	1-800-795-9295

TABLE 2 TOPIC AREAS AND EXAMPLES OF CONTENT FOR THE RESOURCE CENTER FOR YOUNG PARENTS-TO-BE.

TOPIC AREA	EXAMPLES OF CONTENT
Nurturing your newborn	Newborn appearance; crying; use of thermometer and bulb syringe; signs of illness; shaken baby syndrome; swaddling; baby carriers; baby massage
Handling; bathing; diapering	Diaper rash; cord and circumcision care; tub and sponge baths; dressing baby
Safety for babies and young children	Baby-proofing your home; crib safety; first aid; safe positions for baby; car seat safety; immunizations
Guiding children in positive ways; stress reduction for parents; fun with baby	Normal development; use of timeout and other guidance techniques; toilet training; temper tantrums; dealing with stress; songs and finger plays; books for children; what makes a good toy; making songbooks, mobiles, and family albums
Feeding babies from birth to one year	Burping; breastfeeding; bottle-feeding; adding solids; avoiding bottlemouth syndrome
Caring for yourself and your baby before birth	Effects of alcohol, smoking, and drugs; nutrition; fetal development; preterm labor and premature babies; fetal models to hold; car safety during pregnancy

Some attended one session only, and others attended up to four, compared to 67 visits by 34 pregnant women and 8 support persons in the previous semester. At the adolescent pregnancy school program, the center recorded 95 visits by 28 pregnant girls during the spring 2000 semester, with some attending one session only and others attending all six. The maximum time spent by any one individual in the past at the resource center was 13 hours over five sessions by a 15-year-old pregnant girl attending prenatal clinics at the health unit.

Other than increasing attendance as an indirect reflection, ample evidence exists that the center is meeting the prospective parents' needs for knowledge about children's needs, development, and care. Evaluation forms completed by the participants included completing the sentence "One thing that I learned in the Center that was *new* information for me," and typical answers were as follows:

- "Mostly everything,"
- "How to position a baby when put to sleep,"
- "Why the baby cries,"
- "The massage techniques,"
- "Car seat safety,"
- "I didn't know a baby likes black and white first,"
- "The latching on while breastfeeding,"
- "How to make my own baby food,"
- "The different and important reasons for breastfeeding,"
- "It's [sic] more to pregnancy than you think,"
- "What alcohol/smoking can do to a baby [fetus],"
- "About the preterm labor and the folic acid,"
- "All the calories in fast food,"
- "The way your fetus looks," and
- "How to care for your child—show them a lot of love and attention."

Answers to the sentence completion "Something that I will do *differently* with my baby as a result of attending this Center" included the following:

- "Everything,"
- "More closeness, might breastfeed,"
- "Pay close attention to reasons for the baby being upset/crying,"
- "Have my home very secure,"
- "By not getting agrivated [sic] so quickly and understanding that it's normal behavior,"
- "Waiting to potty train them until they are ready,"
- "I won't drink, smoke, or do any drugs,"
- "Sing to it,"
- "Talk to my baby in a calm voice,"
- "Don't whip it when it catch [sic] temper tantrums,"
- "Don't whip my grandbaby,"
- "Read to her more often," and
- "Eat more than I used to eat" [pregnant 15-year-old].

FACILITATING EXPERIENTIAL LEARNING

Much organization is required to plan for and facilitate the experiential learning of students in the resource center. Students are divided into six clinical groups of 9 to 10 students per group at the beginning of the semester. Within the first few weeks, students are given handouts explaining the resource center and their teaching role in it and are further oriented in class. At this time, each clinical group is assigned to one of the six topic areas with dates designated to provide help for the resource center at the health unit and for the adolescent pregnancy program. All resource center experiences are scheduled in the second half of the semester in order to allow sufficient time for student mastery of assigned content material and teaching materials and of maternal-child content in general.

Students are provided with an Every Touch Counts teaching manual and a sheet (see Figure 1) that lists the resource center activity stations for their group's topic area, the teaching materials provided, instructions for teaching, and applicable readings from the course textbook. Student questions or concerns are addressed by the instructor as they arise, and the teaching materials are available for student examination and practice prior to the clinical assignments. For example, students who will be demonstrating the use of baby carriers are expected to be proficient in their use prior to their resource center assignments; students who will be using games such as "Food Pyramid Bingo" and the "Fetus Game" need to have read the rules to know how the games are played.

Teaching materials and activity stations are designed to promote interaction between nursing students and resource center participants. Each resource center topic area has between 11 and 16 numbered activity stations with learning strategies such as hands-on visual aids (for example, dolls, bathtubs, and fetal models), puzzles and quizzes, games, videos, brochures, flip charts, and posters to discuss. Free or purchased materials were obtained from various sources (Table 1). Although students are told that all materials are provided, many have contributed materials of their own design, such as posters and handouts, thus broadening their experiential learning experience.

The students help transport materials to and from the clinical site and set up the resource center at the site. Each student is paired with one or two participants to complete the learning activities that the participants choose. They introduce themselves to the participants who enter the center and help them complete the registration procedure before proceeding to the activities with them. The instructor is available for questions and guidance and circulates in the resource center to observe student-participant interactions and to offer suggestions when appropriate. Most students prepare themselves thoroughly for this assignment and are able to utilize the activities well to facilitate learning among the resource center participants.

ADOPTING A PERSPECTIVE OF RECIPROCITY

The students are encouraged during their class orientation to treat center participants with respect and as partners in their own care and are encouraged to talk *with* them rather than *at* them during the sessions. Evaluative comments from clients that support the student's success in enacting this facet of reciprocity include the following:

- "They take their time with you—they don't rush you,"
- ". . . everyone [was] so patient, helpful, and friendly,"
- "I had a nice teacher guiding me through,"
- "The room was fill [sic] with happiness,"

FIGURE 1	EXAMPLE OF AN INSTRUCTION SHEET GIVEN TO NURSING STUDENTS

The University of Louisiana at Lafayette, College of Nursing & Allied Health Professions
Nursing 301—Instructions for Students Assigned to Resource Center for Parents-To-Be

Topic—Handling, Bathing, and Diapering

ACTIVITIES PARTICIPANTS CAN CHOOSE	TEACHING MATERIALS NEEDED	STUDENT INSTRUCTIONS FOR TEACHING (NOTE: Do not actually apply lotion, powder, water, etc. to dolls). Readings: See Wong and Perry (W&P), & Lesson 2 in Every Touch Counts handbook.
1. Practice diapering a baby (disposable and cloth).	Doll, disposable and cloth diapers, diaper pins in a bar of soap, rubber pants, baby powder and lotion, baby wipes, baby washcloth, blue sheetsaver, diaper pail, small toy, and "poster" (sheet) on "How to Change a Diaper"	Use Lesson 2 content on diapering (4 pgs) to teach the concepts of organization, safety, and loving treatment of baby. Lead participants through two diaper changes (disposable and cloth), helping or advising as needed. Teach safe use of powder (shake into hand away from baby, *then* put on baby, to keep baby from breathing it in). Do not cover cord and circumcision care and care of diaper rash if participants have already done those activities. Ask participants to list some advantages and disadvantages for both disposable and cloth diapers, and ask what they've decided to use. Make sure that participants can show you how they'd fold a cloth diaper to fit the baby. Show them (1) how to twist the cloth diaper at the crotch when they put it on so that it fits better and is double thickness at the crotch, (2) how keeping the diaper pins in a bar of soap makes them slide more easily into the fabric of the diaper, (3) how to put the diaper pin in so that the point is *away* from the baby's abdomen, and (4) how to put two diapers together before folding for an older baby or for the nighttime diaper. Talk about distracting an older baby with a small toy during the diaper change. Mention that store brands of baby products are less expensive and just as good as name brands (e.g., Equate is the Wal-Mart brand).

Objective	Materials	Instructions
2. Learn what to do for diaper rash.	Undiapered doll, diaper rash ointment (with zinc oxide), petroleum jelly, blue sheetsaver or diaper, poster "Understanding Your Baby's Skin," and easel	Use Lesson 2 content on diaper rash (one paragraph) and two boxes from poster on diaper rash. Show the participant what zinc oxide looks like and why it and petroleum jelly work. Demonstrate with undiapered doll and sheetsaver or diaper how to put baby on abdomen to expose bottom to air (not if sleeping, though).
3. Learn cord care and circumcision care.	Alcohol, cotton balls, petroleum jelly, 4 × 4 gauze squares, and doll	Use Lesson 2 content on cord care and circumcision care (two paragraphs). Use content from p. 648 of W&P ("Care of the cord") to teach signs of infection and how and why to fold the diaper down to expose the cord. Use content from W&P p. 655 under "Care of the newly circumcised penis" (second paragraph) to teach care of circumcision site.
4. Discuss the "circumcision decision" with a student.	American Academy of Pediatrics' brochures "Circumcision: Information for Parents" and "Care of the Uncircumcised Penis"	Ask participants if they've made a decision yet and what their decision is based on. Go over with the participant some of the advantages and disadvantages from the brochure and W&P that they need to consider to make an *informed* decision. Make sure that they understand that this decision is theirs to make, not a decision that the doctor or hospital makes. Give participants the two brochures. Go over information on the care of the uncircumcised penis.
5. Review a poster on tub and sponge bathing.	Laminated poster "How to Bathe Your Baby," white poster "Bathing," and two table easels	Either go over the posters with the participants or let them read them themselves (whatever they like). Discuss the major concepts with the participants. The laminated poster recommends the use of cotton-tip swabs for the nose—I would not recommend this because of the potential for injury.

FIGURE 1 Continued

Activities participants can choose	Teaching materials needed	Student instructions for teaching (NOTE: Do not actually apply lotion, powder, water, etc. to dolls). Readings: See Wong and Perry (W&P), & Lesson 2 in Every Touch Counts handbook.
6. Practice tub bathing.	Baby tub, towel, washcloth, bath puppet, baby soap, fresh diaper and clothing, doll, blue sheetsaver or second towel, cotton balls, "poster" on "Tub Bath" from Every Touch Counts—Lesson 2, sample bottles of Johnson's baby wash, and handouts with coupons	Encourage participants to do activity #5 first. Guide participants through a tub bath, offering suggestions and praise when appropriate. Encourage participants to talk to the baby during the bath. Remind that tub bath is not appropriate until umbilicus and circumcision have healed. Give participants a sample bottle and a handout with coupon.
7. Practice giving a sponge bath.	Towel, washcloth, bath puppet, baby soap, fresh diaper and clothing, doll, blue sheetsaver or second towel, cotton balls, "poster" on "Sponge Bath" from Every Touch Counts—Lesson 2	Encourage participants to do activity #5 first. Guide participants through a sponge bath, offering suggestions and praise when appropriate. Encourage participants to talk to the baby during the bath. Remind that tub bath is not appropriate until umbilicus and circumcision have healed.
8. Demonstrate how to shampoo a baby's head and take care of cradle cap.	Doll, tub, blanket or towel, baby soap, small brush, fine-tooth comb, soft toothbrush from baby grooming set, and poster "Understanding Your Baby's Skin"	Demonstrate how to wash baby's head (see photo p. 647 of W&P)—this is the best way to wash a small baby's head). Use information on cradle cap from W & P p. 648 (under "Bathing the baby") and from box on cradle cap on poster to teach what to do.

9. Learn how to cut a baby's nails.	Doll and small nail clippers and scissors from baby grooming set	Suggest cutting a baby's nails while the baby is sleeping. Demonstrate how to immobilize a baby's fingers so that you can cut the nails safely.
10. Try putting clothes on a doll.	Doll in diaper, diaper shirt, all-in-one, blanket, and light green booklet "Clothes for Newborns Through Seven Years"	See tips on p. 648 of W&P under "Dressing the infant" and three paragraphs in Lesson 2 for what to teach the participants as they dress the doll. Remind them to always support the baby's head when handling the baby, because the neck muscles are not strong enough to hold the head up. See if participants know how to swaddle the baby in a blanket. If they don't know how, ask why they think swaddling works (fetus is in a "swaddled" position in the uterus, so many newborns are comforted by swaddling), and lead them through swaddling the doll (see drawing on p. 639 W&P rather than description in Lesson 1). Show participants the booklet; if they are interested, they can look at it with you (the starred areas are the most important).
11. Complete word find puzzle "Bathe the Baby."	Word find puzzle "Bathe the Baby" (pink paper), pencils, and stickers	Give participants a copy of the puzzle and a pencil. Go over it to see if they got all 12 words. Give them a sticker of their choice! (They can keep the puzzle).

- "They work with you and walk you through everything,"
- "The people are understanding and also considerate,"
- "They talk to you like you're an adult not like a little kid," and
- "It's nice to hear information from people that are learning also instead of being preached at by some expert."

The behavior of many of the women changes once they are in the center with the students. Though initially closed and guarded in their expressions, many "open up" and disclose their concerns and needs to the students once they begin to know and trust them.

Because each person's feedback is important in a reciprocal relationship, an evaluation form is offered to all participants to complete before they leave the center. The forms are examined for trends by the students and the instructor during post-conferences, and the students' reports about participants' verbal comments are also considered. The feedback is used whenever possible to meet the needs of the participants more closely. For example, the original format for the teaching project was a set of four traditionally taught 1 1/4-hour classes on each of six dates during the semester (two in the morning and two in the afternoon), with one name pulled for a small door prize at each class. Participants let us know that they were willing to attend morning but not afternoon classes, that the classes needed to be shortened, and that the classes needed to be rotated so that topics would fall in the morning instead of the afternoon all of the time. These changes were made during the first two years of the teaching project.

A total redesign was considered in the fourth semester of the project. Participants had indicated that they wanted more one-on-one interaction with the students, less lecture format, more hands-on experience with models and other audiovisual tools, briefer learning experiences to fit their timetables, more flexibility in time of attendance during the day, and more tangible rewards for their participation. When a resource center format was proposed and described, with points toward gifts of their choosing being awarded for time spent in the center, the participants were unanimously positive. It has been found that the one-on-one resource center model fosters reciprocity much more than the previous traditional class model.

Another aspect of reciprocity is that the community members who participate have a choice of activities within the resource center; for example, in the session called "Nurturing Your Newborn," women who have already mastered use of a thermometer and bulb syringe often prefer to focus on other activities such as use of baby carriers and baby massage. Additionally, if more pressing concerns are apparent, the nursing students are free to address them with the participant. One teen participant approaching the end of her pregnancy wanted to talk about childbirth with her assigned student to ease her fears and to correct misinformation.

And lastly, reciprocity can also mean that the nursing student may learn as much about content, process, and the population with which they are working as the community member who participates in the service learning project. One notable example was a Mexican mother who shared with students the child-rearing traditions of her culture, including the concepts of extended breastfeeding, decreased dependence on physicians for minor ailments with use of home remedies instead, and their view of circumcision as unnecessary and disfiguring.

REFLECTING ON THEIR EXPERIENCES

After each resource center session, the instructor conducts a post-conference with the students to allow reflection. In addition, students are asked to enter into their clinical journals a critique of their resource center teaching and observations they make of psychosocial changes of pregnancy in the women who participate. Philosophical or theoretical issues as well as practical questions are brought up; for example, one student who had taught a mother-translator pair wondered whether he should have looked more at the mother or the translator when talking. Students often are surprised at how competent they feel in their newly acquired teaching role and at how much more confidence they possess during their second resource center experience. Those who think they have nothing to offer because of their lack of personal experience with parenting realize that they "know" more about parenting and child care than some of the multiparous women they assist. Many of the women, for example, are unaware of the technique of timeout for disciplining a child until they learn it from a student in the resource center. Students are dismayed to find that what they consider general basic information in their own socioeconomic milieu is not basic information in other groups. The complexities and integral role of teaching in maternal-child care are better appreciated after this service learning experience.

Because some students are woefully unaware of the extent of the state's problem with adolescent pregnancy, they are astounded to see the numbers of pregnant adolescents at the school site (an average of 16 per session). Some post-conferences are devoted to the strategies they, as future nursing and community leaders, would use to decrease the teen pregnancy rate. Students have been able to discuss with the adolescents their support systems and have concluded that support is inadequate for many adolescents. One clinical group suggested that the course develop a mentoring program, with each student being paired with a pregnant teen who could call for information or support when needed.

Early in the establishment of the resource center, one clinical group decided that instead of each student being responsible for one or two learning activities, that it would be more productive and satisfying for each student to shepherd one or two women or adolescents through *all* of the chosen activities. They realized that this pairing would allow trust to develop between the participant and the student and that the student would thus be more able to meet the participant's needs. An added benefit to the student is the increased content mastered.

Other suggestions that have emerged during post-conference or have appeared in students' clinical journals include asking the class to clip coupons for baby items to give to the pregnant women, purchasing additional needed visual aids such as a cloth breast model and breast pump, and omitting films and quizzes for the teens who dislike these strategies because of their resemblance to school activities. Also, students are aware that many women are unfamiliar with community resources as commonly known as the public library. One student group suggested a resource table with items such as dates of hospital prenatal classes, information on government programs such as WIC, lists of recommended books on birth and parenting issues that are available at the library, and important phone numbers (for example, Poison Control, 232-HELP, and Women's and Children's Health Information Center).

SUMMARY AND CONCLUSIONS

The Resource Center for Young Parents-To-Be has proven to be a valuable service learning project not only for the pregnant girls and women it serves, but also for the nursing students who staff it. The community participants receive essential knowledge about their children's needs, development, and care, which may help prevent child neglect and abuse. The experiential learning assists the students to develop the teaching role of the nurse, to appreciate the reciprocal nature of the nurse-client relationship, and to use critical thinking skills to reflect on their experiences in the resource center.

REFERENCES

Jacoby, B. (1996). *Service-learning in higher education: Concepts and practices*. San Francisco: Jossey-Bass.

Louisiana Children's Trust Fund. (1997). A *child abuse prevention plan* 1997–1999. Baton Rouge, LA: Bourque Printing.

CHAPTER

SERVICE LEARNING IN THE SCHOOL SETTING: OBESITY MANAGEMENT IN PREADOLESCENT CHILDREN

Lisa Broussard

Community-based pediatric nursing education provides students with an excellent opportunity to implement the concepts of service learning. The University of Louisiana at Lafayette College of Nursing and Allied Health Professions benefits greatly from a community partnership with local school nurses and school-based health centers. Pediatric nursing faculty recognize elementary and middle schools as clinical sites that have great potential for enriching student nurse experiences. Due to the inadequate number of school nurses and resources available for health education in the school system, this is an area that greatly benefits from the services and health education provided by baccalaureate nursing students and faculty along with other university students.

In 1995, the Pew Health Professions Commission recommended the following:

- development of programs at the various levels of nursing education that reflect the contributions needed in the changing client care system
- restructuring of faculty positions in nursing schools and programs to involve them more directly with the client care system and nursing practice
- redirection of a significant part of all nursing programs and schools to the health care needs of community-based clients
- implementation of comprehensive and ongoing programs of strategic planning within each nursing school and program

The strategies and recommendations of the commission are readily apparent in the programs conducted by the college in the school setting. Hales (1997) defined service learning as "an approach to education in which relevant community service experiences are integrated with academic course learning" (p. 15). The school setting provides an ideal opportunity for the provision of community services as a component of learning at the baccalaureate level.

The school-based health centers that are utilized for clinical experiences provide services to children from three to twenty years of age enrolled in public schools in a rural, medically underserved area of southwest Louisiana. The majority of these children have no physician for provision of primary health care. In emergency situations, most of these children obtain care in the emergency room of the state-owned hospital 30 miles away. Therefore, these students rely greatly on services provided by the school-based health centers. A part-time physician, full-time pediatric nurse practitioner, registered nurse, social worker, and Medicaid specialist are employed by each of the three health centers in the parish. Parental consent is obtained for all services and for the administration of over-the-counter medications. Baccalaureate nursing students attend the health center for one day of their pediatric rotation with a faculty member and provide primary care under standing orders from the medical director of the clinic. They also attend the school-based health center for one day with the pediatric nurse practitioner, which provides them with the opportunity to observe an advanced practice nurse in a community setting.

In 1998, the nurse practitioner working in the school-based health centers recognized that large numbers of children seen at the health center were obese, a finding that is consistent with a national trend. Obesity is one of the most significant health problems in the United States today, and the number of seriously overweight children and adolescents has more than doubled in the last three decades. It is estimated that almost 30% of children and teens are overweight, and the numbers appear to be rising. An overweight adolescent has a 70% chance of becoming an obese adult, and obesity can lead to a higher risk of life-threatening health problems, including hypertension, premature heart disease, and diabetes. Aside from the physical risks, overweight children can exhibit emotional ramifications secondary to peer ridicule and labeling, jeopardizing their self-esteem (Sothern, 1999). In examining the high incidence of childhood obesity in children served by the school-based health centers and the lack of resources available within the system to address this issue, the baccalaureate pediatric faculty developed an obesity health education program, which was implemented by nursing students.

In 1998, an instructional mini-grant was awarded to the pediatric faculty for funding of this program. Nursing faculty solicited the assistance of faculty from the Dietetics Department for development of the program. The goal of the Obesity Management Health Education Program was to introduce overweight school-age children to concepts of healthy eating (including food labels, the food guide pyramid, and the importance of a low fat, high fiber diet), the importance of exercise, and self-esteem issues related to their weight.

During the fall 1999 semester, the program was implemented. Health center staff identified 10 obese children who were between the ages of 10 and 12 for participation, and parental consent was obtained. The program consisted of six sessions with the children over a period of four weeks. Five "stations" were set up—aerobics, stretching, self-esteem, demographics (weight, height, and body fat analysis), and nutrition—and the actual teaching at each station was conducted by the nursing students and dietetic interns. Children spent 10 to 12 minutes at each station, with activity logs and dietary recalls integrated into each session. This format prevented the children from becoming bored with one area and allowed for interactive learning. One of the sessions included parent participation, and the final session consisted of a party, with the dietetic interns demonstrating the preparation of healthy snacks. Each participant was awarded a plaque for participation, which proved to be very exciting for them, since many had never received a plaque or trophy before. Weight loss, although not an expected outcome over such a short period of time, was experienced by four of the participants. It is unclear whether the weight loss was a result of the program or not, although a posttest did indicate that the children had increased their knowledge related to principles of healthy eating and the importance of exercise. Referrals to the social worker were made for those children who demonstrated the need for counseling. The overweight children, the nursing students, and the dietetic interns all enjoyed the program immensely. Upon completion of the program, the health center nurse and the nurse practitioner continued to follow these children on a weekly or biweekly basis, monitoring their weight and reinforcing what had been introduced during the Obesity Management Program.

The Kellogg Faculty Committee on Service Learning at the University of Michigan described six features of service learning, which are readily apparent with the Obesity Management Health Education Program.

1. Service learners apply knowledge by testing and applying academic learning. Baccalaureate nursing students received the concepts of health education, school-age growth and development, and principles of nutrition and obesity in the didactic portion of nursing and nutrition classes. Application of these principles in the school setting allowed for transfer of knowledge and enhanced understanding.
2. Synthesize knowledge by bringing together past and present learning, giving coherence to students' studies. As previously stated, nursing students and dietetic interns were able to practically apply information received from the very beginning of their higher educational experience.
3. Critically think and analyze by learning to distinguish what is and is not important in the unfiltered context of the real world. In accordance with the most recent nursing accreditation standards, which require nursing schools to provide evidence of student achievement of critical thinking (Green, 2000), pediatric faculty recognize the need for advanced reasoning skills in the clinical setting. Distinguishing essential versus nonessential information is crucial to this process. During the Obesity Management Program, the children discussed many issues. The nursing students were responsible for informing the appropriate professionals for follow up as needed (for example, referral was made to the nurse practitioner for an elevated blood pressure and to a social worker for apparent depression). The

nursing students demonstrated the ability to critically analyze each situation and to respond accordingly.

4. Learn about cultural diversity by learning with, from, and about people of other races, ages, economic means, and competencies. The majority of the participants were from a low socioeconomic background, and seven of the ten children were of African American descent. For many of the nursing students, this was their first opportunity to work with children living in impoverished circumstances. The health education program required that the students take into account cultural influences on nutrition, limited resources for the purchase of healthy food, and also the need to incorporate principles of exercise that would require little money. Two of the children were enrolled in special education services for poor academic performance due to learning disabilities, so this had to be incorporated into the teaching plan as well. The school-based health center experience has consistently provided the nursing students with an opportunity to experience cultural diversity, which is unique for many of them.

5. Develop values with first-hand interaction with community issues. The sensitive nature of obesity required the students to portray sensitivity and compassion in conducting each lesson. The self-esteem issues that were discussed allowed the nursing students as well as the overweight children to examine their feelings and values concerning the complexity associated with weight in modern society.

6. Learn inductive reasoning by using the specific as an embarkation point for hypothesizing and theorizing. This experience allowed nursing students to learn principles of formal health education that can be applied to various clinical settings. They also learned techniques for communicating with the school-age population. This experience as a whole provided them with valuable skills that can be applied to many clinical sites.

The Obesity Management Health Education Program is an excellent example of service learning in a select community. The baccalaureate Department of Nursing will implement this program again during the spring 2000 semester at another rural school health center. Schools are excellent examples of settings in which nursing students and faculty can collaborate with other disciplines to provide much needed health education programs and interventions to improve the overall health of those children with limited access to services.

REFERENCES

Green, C. (2000). *Critical thinking in nursing*. New Jersey: Prentice-Hall.

Hales, A. (1997). Service learning within the nursing curriculum. *Nurse Educator, 22*, 15–18.

Pew Health Professions Commission. (1995). *Critical challenges: Revitalizing the health professions for the twenty-first century*. San Francisco: UCSF Center for Health Professions.

Sothern, M. (1999). http://www.committed-to-kids.com.

CHAPTER

SERVICE LEARNING IN THE PEDIATRIC COMMUNITY SETTING: IMMUNIZATION CLINIC

Susan W. Reynolds

Students enrolled in the nursing curriculum at the University of Louisiana at Lafayette are exposed on a continuous basis to the educational value of clinical experience in conjunction with classroom theory and didactics. As early as their first semester junior year, the nursing students are involved in a wide variety of clinical activities where service learning is applied.

Service learning has received widespread recognition in current literature. The definition of service learning, however, can vary depending on the source. Regardless, at its core, service learning is a form of experiential learning that employs service as its "modus Operandi" (Crews, 1995, p. 1).

> The basic theory of service-learning is Dewey's: the interaction of knowledge and skills with experience is key to learning. Students learn best not by reading the Great Books in a closed room but by opening the doors and windows of experience. Learning starts with a problem and continues with the application of increasingly complex ideas and increasingly sophisticated skills to increasingly complicated problems. (Erlich, 1996, p. 11)

The concept of service learning has been successfully implemented by teachers in colleges and universities as well as in K–12 schools to enhance traditional modes of learning.

So what exactly is service learning? One source describes it as an approach to education whereby relevant community service experiences are integrated with academic and classroom course learning (Howard, 1993). The merger of community service and classroom learning strengthens both and generates a whole that is greater than the sum of its parts. Service is improved by having a foundation in the curriculum, and learning is increased by using the community as a laboratory for the classroom where students can test and apply their curriculum in real-life situations (Stephens, 1995). Since learning can be further intensified by reflection, students should be required to contemplate the meaning of their service and evaluate its impact on themselves and on the population served. As a result, they will reach a greater understanding of themselves and the society in which they live.

Cognitive theories have for many years postulated that direct experience and reflection are both essential for effective learning. David Kolb (1984) has theorized that learning requires four steps: observe or experience events, reflect on that experience, develop concepts that explain and allow generalizations from the events, and then test these concepts in a variety of situations. These four steps are able to be readily implemented in service learning situations. The concept of service learning was developed partly as an expression of the benefits thought to be associated with the experience-based learning model (Alt & Medrich, 1994).

A distinction is made between community service and service learning in the literature. Community service may be added to the curriculum, while "Service learning is an innovative concept. It is not simply a field trip to a soup kitchen. Service learning involves students in meeting real human needs as part of the school curriculum, enabling them to learn by doing" (Stephens, 1995, p. 2).

Service learning has been an integral part of the nursing curriculum at the University of Louisiana for many years. The faculty at the College of Nursing and Allied Health Sciences have long recognized the benefit of service learning to both the student and to the community at large. Service learning increases retention for many students and increases the relevancy of their education to what actually occurs in the "real world." It allows the student to explore careers and majors and to develop occupational skills, and it teaches positive values, leadership, citizenship and personal responsibility. In addition, it increases tolerance and acceptance of diversity. Personal growth and self-image is enhanced, and in many students a sense of social responsibility and commitment to public service is fostered. The university as a whole also benefits from service learning, for it contributes to a university's outreach efforts to the local community and to the state. Increased campus-community collaborations and partnerships are also fostered, and community education is increased. In addition, countless hours of service are contributed to people in need, to nonprofit agencies, and to governmental agencies, to name just a few recipients of service learning.

As stated previously, students begin to operationalize the concept of service learning in the first semester of their junior year while enrolled in N-301, Nursing Care of Children and the Childbearing Family. Students participate in several clinics offered by the Lafayette Parish Health Unit, including Immunization Clinic, Specialty Clinics devoted to children with various chronic diseases, and Maternity Clinic. In addition, students participate in several school-based health clinics in the community and surrounding area.

The remainder of this chapter will focus on the immunization clinic service learning activity in which all first-semester junior nursing students participate. The Lafayette Parish Health Unit offers both childhood and adult immunizations to the public at large three afternoons a week. Nursing students have been participating in this particular activity for approximately ten years.

Each nursing student spends one clinical day at the immunization clinic with a clinical instructor. Nursing students are assigned to the clinic in groups of five. Prior to attending the clinic, students have received the following:

1. theory and practice in a learning resource lab on actual administration of intramuscular and subcutaneous injections
2. principles of growth and development from birth to the older adult in the didactic portion of nursing and psychology classes
3. principles of health promotion and disease prevention and specific information on immunizations available to the public
4. learning objectives for the immunization clinic experience

Once at the clinic, students along with the clinical instructor participate in all phases of the immunization clinic. Initially, the students assess each client to determine immunization history, allergies, and current health status. A determination is then made as to what immunizations are needed on this particular visit to the clinic. This is perhaps one of the most challenging aspects of the clinic as there are many mandated vaccines and specific time schedules to be followed that are required by law for children and adolescents. Once this determination has been made, the nursing students then counsel the parents on the vaccines that the client will be receiving and expected side effects. Once the student is satisfied that the parent has an understanding of this information, the actual vaccines are administered by the student. For the majority of the nursing students, this is the first time they have administered any type of injection to a client. Once the vaccines have been administered, the student completes the necessary paperwork and gives the client a return appointment if needed. Nursing students rotate through this process with the clinical instructor in attendance.

Following the clinic, the five students and clinical instructor meet to reflect on the day's activities and to discuss any issues or concerns of the students or instructor. In addition, the students complete a written assignment and journal related to the experience.

In the spring 2000 semester, questionnaires were distributed to the parents of 23 of the clients following their experience at the Lafayette Parish Health Unit with the nursing students to assess their level of satisfaction with their visit. The following six questions were asked of the respondents:

1. Have you or any members of your immediate family been cared for before by students from the University of Louisiana at Lafayette College of Nursing and Allied Health Professions? If so, could you describe this experience? Was it a positive or negative experience?

2. How would you describe your experience with the nursing students today?
3. Were you and your family treated today in an efficient, professional manner?
4. Were your questions and concerns adequately addressed today?
5. How would you compare the care you received today from the nursing students to that you have received from the public health nurses in the past?
6. How could your experience today be improved for future families?

Thirty-four questionnaires were returned to the clinical instructor. Twenty-nine (85%) of the respondents had not received any previous care by nursing students from the College of Nursing and Allied Health Professions. Five respondents (15%) had previously received care by nursing students and stated it had been a positive experience. One respondent specifically commented that student nurses had assisted with the birth of her baby at University Medical Center in Lafayette and that they were polite and professional as well as compassionate.

When the parents or caregivers were asked to describe their experience with the nursing students at the immunization clinic, their responses were overwhelmingly positive. Examples of specific responses to this question included the following:

- "The nursing students were great; they were caring and concerned about my child's fears."
- "They did a very good job. They were just as good as any other nurse he has been to."
- "A very positive experience; the students were friendly, polite, and conscientious. The instructor was watchful and guided the students who gave the shots every step of the way."
- "The nursing students were extremely caring; they didn't get scared when my child was crying and very upset."
- "The students were very friendly, efficient, and professional."
- "The nursing students were kind and comforting, not to mention quick and confident. Confident nurses give the patient a sense of security."
- "It was a great experience; they were very attentive to both of my children's needs while they got their shots."

All 34 of the respondents (100%) felt that they and their families were treated in an efficient, professional manner. One mother also commented in response to this question that the students were also very kind both to her and to her son. Once again, all 34 of the respondents (100%) felt that the nursing students at the clinic adequately addressed their questions and concerns.

When the parents or caregivers were asked to compare the care they received by the nursing students to that they may have received from the public health nurses in the past, the following comments were elicited:

- "The students were friendlier and more compassionate. We didn't feel like we were just another person there for a shot."
- "The nursing students were so much more patient. They worked with each patient individually, not treating them like a whole group of patients."
- "The students were actually friendlier and more attentive than some of the nurses I have come across."
- "The students showed more caring. "
- "The students were excellent, better than most of the nurses."
- "The care was exactly the same; the nursing students were informative."
- "The nursing students were more interested in what was going on than the public health nurses."

In response to the final question asked of the caregivers—"How could your experience be improved for future families?"—the following comments were made:

- "No improvement necessary; everything was done as well as possible."
- "It was perfect; nothing should be changed."
- "It was great, good job; I don't see any need for improvement."
- "Needs no improvement; my experience was very good."
- "My experience was very good. I don't know where there is need for improvement."

In this same spring 2000 semester, a questionnaire was distributed to the nursing students following their experience at the immunization clinic. The following five questions were asked of the students:

1. Prior to your enrollment in N-301, what knowledge did you have of community programs available to the pediatric community in Lafayette, Louisiana?
2. Do you feel that the information you now have about community resources will be of benefit to you in your career? If so, could you describe briefly how you feel it may be helpful?
3. Overall, how would you describe the community-based experiences (positive, negative), and why?
4. What insights have you gained from the individual clients and families you have cared for and interacted with in the community-based experiences?
5. How do you feel the community-based experiences could be improved?

Twenty-two questionnaires were returned from the nursing students. Eleven of the respondents (50%) had no previous knowledge of community resource programs available to the pediatric population in our region. The other 11 of the respondents (50%) stated that they did have some previous knowledge of resources available. One student stated that she had knowledge of some community programs but did not know about all of the services they provided until she actually attended them. Another student commented that she did know about the Lafayette Public Health Unit, as she received her immunizations there as a child. Finally, one student commented that she knew immunizations were available for the pediatric population, but she did not know where one went for them or what the cost was to the families.

All 22 of the respondents (100%) felt that the information they now had about the various community resources would be of benefit to them in their careers. Comments elicited in response to this question included the following:

- "I can now refer clients to different clinics and suggest resources they can use that they might not have been aware of."
- "I feel that the information I now have about community resources will help me when I do patient/parent education. I will be able to tell clients about services they may be eligible to receive."
- "Now, if I encounter a difficult situation where I believe an outside resource may be needed, I feel that I have some knowledge about where I can refer such a client. If a client has a need for services or knowledge that I cannot help with, I am glad that I now know of some community resources that I can refer them to."
- "Since I am now more informed about community resources, I can relay this to clients that are in need of these services in the future. I feel more confident in educating and questioning clients in order to promote their well-being."

All 22 of the nursing students (100%) felt that the community-based experiences were positive. Comments related to this question included the following:

- "I was able to gain more experience in working with patients in the community; it helped to raise my confidence level."
- "This was a very positive experience; you learned a lot about nursing outside of the hospital."
- "The experiences allowed for a lot of hands-on experience."
- "These community experiences have a positive effect on our learning. They give us, the students, the opportunity to see a variety of nursing options as well as let us know that these resources exist for our own benefit as well as our clients."
- "The experiences were very positive; the nurses were helpful, and it was interesting to work with a variety of clients."
- "Our clinical instructors guided us through the experiences, and everything was done in an orderly manner."
- "It was positive in that I learned so much about the community that I live in and the various health problems present in the community."

Insights gained by the nursing students from the community-based experiences included the following:

- "I have learned how to interact with people of all socioeconomic levels and with different cultural backgrounds from my own."
- "We have been able to interact with a wide variety of people in our community, with different races and nationalities, and a wide range of ages. These individuals have had many different needs, and we have had to adjust to all of their differences."
- "I have realized that these community resources really do benefit the population served. Many of these clients don't have the money or transportation to see private medical doctors, so resources like the school-based clinics and immunization clinic really provide a needed service for parents as well as the children."
- "I have learned how to interact and communicate more effectively with clients and also feel like I understand them better as a result of my experiences."
- "I have gained a sense of appreciation from these families. They were pleased with the caring attitudes we displayed toward their families."
- "The most important thing that I have learned from the patients and families that I have cared for is that nurses must follow the cardinal rule: They must care about each patient as though they were the one being care for."

When asked how the community experiences could be improved, many of the students had no suggestions. A few, however, had the following comments:

- "I liked it the way it was, but it could be beneficial if we could spend more time in these experiences, especially the immunization clinic."
- "I feel that the experiences could be improved by focusing on the everyday nursing skills that we need to know and not focusing as much time on the paper work that needs to be done."
- "I think the only way that it could be improved is by getting the information out, so more people know about the community resources. Another problem is that often once the clients come to the clinics, they have to wait a long time to be seen. Efforts should be made to shorten client waiting time."

One student also commented that she would have liked more than one day in each community experience.

As a result of their participation in the immunization clinic, many of the nursing students have gone on to volunteer for the Shots for Tots program that is conducted by three of the hospital medical centers in the Lafayette area. This program, which was started approximately five years ago to offer working parents the opportunity to have their children immunized on a Saturday morning, is offered by each of the three hospitals once a month. Nursing students have volunteered for this additional activity and have found it to be a rewarding experience.

In conclusion, the incorporation of service learning in the nursing curriculum has been a positive experience both for the student and the clients and caregivers served. Students gain a deeper understanding of the diversity of the population served, improve their communication skills, and gain actual hands-on experience with a wide variety of clients. Students gain knowledge of career options available to them and increase their knowledge of community services, which can help foster their careers. The clients and their caregivers also benefit from the nursing student's participation in community programs. Parents and caregivers found the students to be very caring, knowledgeable, and patient. Questions and concerns were adequately addressed by the students and in many cases in more detail than that provided by the public health nurses themselves.

REFERENCES

Alt, M., & Medrich, E. (1994). Student outcomes from participation in community service." *http://www.quest.edu/slarticle13.htm*.

Crews, R. (1995, April). What is Service-learning? In *University of Colorado at Boulder Service-Learning Handbook* (1st ed.). Boulder, CO.

Ehrlich, T. (1996). Forward learning in higher education: Concepts and practices. In B. Jacoby and Associates, *Service* (pp. xi–xii). San Francisco: Jossey-Bass.

Howard, J. (1993). Advocating for community service learning at the University of Michigan. In J. Galvra et al (Eds.), *Praxis II: Service-Learning Resources for University Students, Staff, and Faculty.* (pp. 39–54). Ann Arbor, MI: The Office of Community Service-Learning Press.

Kolb, D. (1984). *Experiential learning: Experience as the source of learning and development.* Englewood Cliffs, NJ: Prentice-Hall.

Stephens, L. (1995). *The complete guide to learning through community service: Grades K-9.* Des Moines, IA: Allyn & Bacon.

SERVICE LEARNING WITH VULNERABLE POPULATION GROUPS IN THE COMMUNITY

Dr. Jerry L. White

Nursing education at the baccalaureate level has long emphasized the concept of service to individuals and groups in the community. Students have learned community nursing knowledge and skills through clinical experiences in local health departments, public school settings, industrial clinics, and in clients' homes. The recent national emphasis on community-based service learning is a natural expansion of nursing's traditional community emphasis, but it is an expansion and it does require a different teaching approach by the nurse educator, a different learning approach by the student, and a supportive administration.

Although the concept of service learning in higher education has been promoted since at least the 1970s (Sigmon, 1979), the 1993 National Community and Service Trust Act (Serow, Calleson, Parker, & Morgan, 1996) and the national 1990 "points of light" program (Marulio, 1996) launched the current emphasis on service learning in higher education. Beginning with the assumption that many young people feel alienated from their communities and thus feel little civic pride or civic responsibility, service learning programs have sought to provide a structured method for reconnecting young adults to their communities in a way that is meaningful to both the student and the community. Meyers (1999) describes several premises of service learning. First, service learning experiences give students the opportunity to actively participate in organized service experiences that meet real community needs. These experiences are planned and coordinated by both the educational institution and the community. Second, service learning experiences incorporate structured time and methods for reflection on the meaning of the service experience for the student. And third, service learning experiences provide opportunities for students to develop a sense of caring for others by using their knowledge and skills to meet community needs in real-life situations.

The basic premises of the community-based service learning movement flow easily into the current nursing education emphases on community-based care and critical thinking (Pew Health Professions Commission, 1995; American Association of Colleges of Nursing, 1997). But the service learning model requires a rethinking of traditional teaching and learning methods. Clinical experiences in community health nursing traditionally take students, with instructor supervision, into local health departments to participate in well-child, maternity, and communicable disease clinics. Community health students may be placed with preceptor nurses in home health or public health home visiting experiences. Other clinical sites may include industrial nursing clinics and school settings. In each of these experiences, the students are able to participate in ongoing nursing activities and are able to observe role models of community-based nursing. The instructor for these traditional experiences serves as the mediator between the agency and the students, the interpreter of the experience for the students, and the teacher of content and skills related to community health nursing.

COMMUNITY-BASED SERVICE LEARNING IS DIFFERENT FROM TRADITIONAL CLINICAL EXPERIENCES

Community-based service learning experiences require faculty, students, and administration to expand their focus. Faculty must be willing to leave the traditional sites where students are able to fit into established programs and where faculty involvement is concentrated on supervision and post-conference teaching. Community-based service learning experiences are developed in relation to community needs, and faculty are often required to create new learning experiences in settings that have had no prior nursing or health component. Faculty must use skills in collaboration and persuasion in order to work with community agency personnel in identifying what nurses can contribute to clients in the setting and which services will be provided. Communication and coordination skills are needed to plan with the agency for space, time, equipment or furnishings, and publicity. Faculty must often begin from nothing to focus and structure student experiences that will meet the community's health needs and the students' learning needs. This may require designing client records, setting procedures, developing orientation plans, and publicizing and selling the service to the community. Faculty must coordinate the supplies and equipment required by the experience and must balance the community need for supplies, the student need for clinical practice, and the agency and nursing department budget. During the service learning experience the faculty function as role models and instructors for the students and as health care providers for the clients. The faculty member is often the only health professional in the setting. The faculty also serve as facilitators in guiding students to reflect on their service learning experiences. The faculty member's role in community-based service learning is complex and requires an ability to continuously balance student learning needs with community care needs in a way that benefits both the student and the community.

Since service learning sites are often in nontraditional settings, students are challenged to be flexible in adapting to the needs of the clients and the environment of the site. Whether it is in a homeless shelter or an older adult apartment building, the focus of the experience is to provide caring service to clients by using the nursing knowledge and skills learned in classroom and previous clinical settings. Students are challenged to expand their model of nursing by adding disease prevention and health promotion concepts. They are required to work on therapeutic communication skills in order to assist clients in setting realistic goals and in order to communicate health information in a way clients can understand. Procedures and interventions must be adapted to the setting, and supplies must be used wisely. Teamwork and time management are required to adapt to space, time, and equipment needs. Students must strengthen critical thinking skills to not only make accurate assessments and provide needed services and referrals but also to think through their own learning. They must be willing to think about how their own learning needs are being met while they are also meeting the health needs of the clients they serve.

Administrative support is critical in developing an environment conducive to designing and expanding community-based service learning experiences. Faculty must be allowed and encouraged to use their creativity in seeking and developing community sites within curricular objectives. Faculty must also be helped to understand the accrediting and regulatory body guidelines under which these experiences can be developed. Administrative support and expertise is often required to communicate to higher levels of university decision makers why nursing clinical experiences are occurring in these nontraditional sites and how nursing practice is more than physical illness care in an institutional setting. Administrators must acknowledge that since service learning experiences most often occur in created clinical settings, the majority of the equipment and supply needs will initially come from the nursing department budget. Administrators can encourage further development of the service learning model by assisting faculty in writing grants and seeking funds for community-based learning experiences.

HEALTH PROMOTION SERVICE LEARNING EXPERIENCES

Based on the belief that health promotion knowledge and interventions have great potential for increasing the quality of life of any population group and using Pender's Health Promotion Model (Pender, 1996) as a guide, the last-semester senior nursing course at the University of Louisiana at Lafayette has developed health promotion service learning experiences in several areas. Student-client interactions in all settings are grounded in the assumption that individuals have the capacity to enhance their own physical and mental health, regardless of their current state of health or living circumstances. Planned interventions also assume that small successful changes lead to increased self-efficacy that leads to further changes. All services offered by the students and faculty focus on providing the recipients with improved knowledge and skills to manage their own health.

The final clinical course, which combines psychiatric and community health content, has been an ideal base for service learning health promotion experiences in the community. Clinical experiences include campus and community health promotion clinics, formal and informal teaching with vulnerable population groups, and reminiscence groups for older adults. Health promotion is the focus in all of these settings, but specific activities are adapted to the needs of the agency and the population being served. Written objectives require students to (1) interact with clients in a manner that grants dignity, (2) collaborate with agency personnel to address the health needs of the population, (3) identify interagency referrals to provide health promotion and disease prevention services, and (4) offer population-appropriate health promotion services and education to groups and individuals.

Health Promotion Clinics

Faculty-developed health promotion clinics have been created for student experiences in a variety of settings. Village du Lac, a government-subsidized, independent-living apartment village for low-income physically and/or mentally handicapped and the elderly, has served as a community clinical site for over ten years and has provided the model for development of the other clinic experiences. The health promotion clinic at Village du Lac is held on a biweekly basis in two centrally located rooms that have been furnished by the management of the complex. The rooms contain file cabinets, desks, chairs, exam tables, and sinks. Residents are notified of clinic dates through the monthly newsletter circulated by the management, through word of mouth, and by flyers posted by both the management and the nursing faculty. In recent semesters, regular participants have been given appointment times and the assigned student makes a reminder telephone call the night before the clinic. The approximately 30 residents who attend the program are assisted by students in setting short-term, attainable goals based on assessment information and expressed client needs and are given health-related information to help them understand the changes that may be needed. Follow-up appointments are made to assist residents in meeting their goals. Although students rotate in and out of the site every three to four visits, the instructor remains the same and provides continuity. All screening supplies, equipment, and charting and educational materials are provided by the nursing program and are taken to the site by the instructor each clinic day. Small grants from the local Junior League and a local foundation for women have assisted with the cost of supplies and materials for this clinic as well as the other service learning opportunities.

Two additional health promotion clinic sites in the community are held at independent-living apartment complexes for the elderly. At Evangeline Apartments, a converted six-story hotel, the weekly clinic is housed in a vacant apartment designated by the management each semester. The apartment is furnished only with chairs and tables but does contain a bathroom and small kitchen. Again, all supplies, including items like soap, paper towels, toilet paper, and all screening supplies, charting supplies, and equipment, are furnished by the instructor or the nursing program. Providing coffee each week has been found to help draw participants for socialization and informal health teaching, so this is an added expense at this site. Of the 80+ residents of the hotel, the clinic currently reaches more than 50. Reminder calls, a resident who serves as liaison, success in meeting individual goals, assistance with needed referrals, a consistent instructor to provide continuity, and a supportive management have all helped to make this site an excellent service learning experience.

Maison de Goodwill, a smaller independent-living complex for middle-income older adults, is the newest site. The biweekly clinic, held in the chair-and-table-furnished community room, reaches 34 of the 40 residents. Since the educational level of this group is higher than at the other two sites, students are frequently challenged in preparing individualized health teaching on a variety of subjects requested by the residents. Pretesting and posttesting of health promotion attitudes and behaviors using the Health Promoting Lifestyle Profile II (Walker, 1996) is completed here, and students are able to see not only screening test results change, but also health promotion attitudes and behaviors change. All supplies and equipment are provided by the nursing program. As at Evangeline Apartments, reminder telephone calls, a resident liaison, a consistent instructor, and supportive management have made this service learning experience successful for residents and students.

A weekly health promotion service learning clinic known as Wellness Wednesdays was started in 1997 for the university community (White, 1999). Wellness Wednesdays is held each Wednesday afternoon during the fall and spring semesters in a clinic-type setting in the centrally located College of Nursing building. The original target group for the clinic was university faculty and staff, but due to the numbers of drop-in visits by students, the focus has now been expanded to include undergraduate and graduate students. Wellness Wednesdays services include individualized health promotion assessment, using the Health Promotion Lifestyle Profile II (Walker, 1996), and health screening measures of height, weight, percent body fat, body mass index, blood pressure, pulse, blood sugar, cholesterol, and hearing and vision. Services are designed to meet the individual needs and goals of the participants and are structured to provide ongoing evaluation through follow-up appointments. Appropriate health information is provided, and referrals to private physicians or community agencies are made as needed. Clients are encouraged by the nursing students to actively participate in planning for their own health promotion behavior changes. All clinic procedures, surveillance and publicity methods, and charting forms have been created by faculty. All equipment, furnishings, and supplies are provided by the nursing department budget and are supplemented by small grants when available. A consistent presence on campus for three years, a supportive administration, frequent flyer reminders, special campus voice mail announcements, and participants who have reached health promotion goals and share their enthusiasm with others have all contributed to the success of this experience for the nursing students and the campus.

Vulnerable Population Sites

Realizing that in order to understand the vast health and welfare needs of vulnerable population groups in the urban community, students must first go to where these groups live on a daily basis, faculty have structured service learning opportunities that bring the vulnerable populations and the students together in ways that benefit both. Four population groups have been selected: (1) the homeless, (2) detained juveniles, (3) the chronic mentally ill, and (4) abused women and their children. Students rotate in and out of the vulnerable population sites every four weeks, but the same instructor remains and maintains continuity for the agencies and the populations. Students begin to understand the needs of the homeless by conducting weekly health promotion activities at The Well, a day shelter for the homeless. The "guests" at The Well are mostly males between the ages of 30 and 50 but also include single mothers with small children and older adults in need of services. Individualized screening and health counseling, formal health education presentations, basic first aid, and community referrals are some of the methods used by students to understand and meet the needs of the homeless population. Foot assessment clinics, complete with new, clean socks, are a popular activity at The Well and provide a means for informal health teaching and counseling. Among other subjects covered in formal and informal education are communicable disease prevention, ABCs of communal living, managing moods and emotions, and dealing with grief and loss. Any materials used for health education or screening are covered by the instructor, the students, or the nursing budget.

The Juvenile Detention Home is a holding facility that houses up to 36 juveniles who have committed a federal crime and are ordered to remain in custody by the courts. Once a week nursing students interact informally and present formal health promotion topics to the detainees during their school day. Presentation topics include exercise, nutritious diet habits, hygiene, prevention of sexually transmitted diseases, blood-borne pathogens and standard precautions, managing moods and emotions, conflict resolution, stress management and anger, career opportunities, and smoking cessation. Nursing students also work one on one to tutor the detainees who need support in a school assignment. This provides a more private setting for the nursing student to interact as a positive role model with the juvenile. Any materials used for presentations are provided by the instructor or the nursing students.

Faith House is a temporary residence for abused women and children where staff advocates assist the residents in formulating realistic plans to regain independence from their abusers and to repair self-esteem and self-confidence. Nursing students provide weekly health promotion programs on topics such as stress reduction, exercise and relaxation, parenting issues, self-defense, disease prevention, when to see the doctor, childhood illnesses, nutrition, and hygiene. Informal health teaching and role modeling is accomplished as students interact with the residents and their children during work and play activities. Health assessment clinics for the women and children include hearing and vision screening and screening for diabetes and heart disease. Individual assessments are provided on an as needed, per request basis by the instructor and students.

At Les Bon Amis, a daytime activity center, students are given the opportunity to interact with 20 to 30 young adults who live with chronic mental illness. Students participate with the clients in center activities to model social skills and to do informal health teaching. Weekly creative presentations on topics such as stress management, exercise, heart disease prevention, first aid, and personal hygiene give clients health promotion information and enhance self-care skills. Hearing and vision screening and weight and body fat analysis provide further opportunities for education and for referral. All equipment and supplies for presentations and for screening are provided by the instructor, the students, and the nursing program. Space and publicity are provided by the agency.

Reminiscence Groups

In an effort to provide students with a meaningful experience in leading a community group while at the same time providing a therapeutic experience for older adults, three reminiscence groups have been started in community settings. For the last three years these weekly "Remember When" groups of 5 to 15 older adults have been held at Evangeline Apartments for the elderly, Magnolia Place Nursing Home, and at a senior activity center known as The Rosehouse. A community nursing instructor in each site coordinates the group and provides for continuity as student partner groups rotate in and out on a weekly basis. Reminiscence group materials to guide topics and discussions were purchased with a small university-awarded grant and have been expanded through imagination and library and Internet searching by one of the psychiatric nursing faculty. Students prepare for the experience by reading assigned articles (Haight & Burggraf, 1992), reviewing the materials for the topic, and preparing and discussing a plan with the assigned instructor. Topics for a recent semester have included Home Life and School Days, Precious

Moments, Clothes and Hair, Church and Sundays, Farm Life, Home Remedies, Games and Recreation, World War II and the Great Depression, Radio and Telephone, The General Store, and Easter Customs. Publicity by the sponsoring agencies and by word of mouth, name tags with stickers for attendance, and lively group discussions have made this a fun and popular experience with the students and the participants.

BENEFITS OF COMMUNITY-BASED SERVICE LEARNING

Since a major component of the service learning model is a structured time and method for reflection (Hales, 1997), each week students are required to reflect on their clinical experiences in a written "Self-Evaluation." For each experience they are asked to record what they did, what they learned about themselves and their practice as a nurse, and how they met their stated goals for the experience. Students write of how service learning experiences have "opened their eyes" to populations they knew little about or even feared. They use words like "I feel fortunate to have been exposed to these communities and see how people live and how they deal with day-to-day stressors." Students write of the rewarding feeling of having knowledge they can use to help someone live a better life. They marvel at how much they really have learned during their education. Students comment on the feeling of professional independence and satisfaction they feel when working with clients who view them as nurses, not students. As one student wrote, "I like the independence. I'm actually beginning to feel like a nurse." Students learn to value what clients can give back to them. Following a reminiscence group, one student wrote, "I realized that you can learn so much from the elderly because they have experienced a lot through the years and they love sharing their experiences with us."

The populations served by the community-based experiences receive low cost or free health screening and health education services that are tailored to their needs. This is the obvious benefit. Since faculty approach each population initially with a request for the population to assist in educating the students about community needs, the participants often feel they are having a part in the student's learning. Some have even stated, "I'm only here to help them, because I don't need anything." Participants who meet their individual health promotion goals often credit the "caring young people" and the regular encouragement of the students for their success. Many say that clinic days offer them an opportunity to get to know their neighbors and to feel they are using their time constructively.

For faculty, a community-based service learning curriculum provides a way to be creative and innovative in meeting student needs and community needs. Because of all of the groundwork required in establishing and maintaining these experiences, faculty are able to form long-term relationships with agency personnel and feel a connection with the community. Since clients often participate for several semesters, faculty are frequently rewarded by seeing positive health behavior and health status changes over time. Faculty in service learning settings essentially have a health promotion clinical practice as they guide the students and the clients in setting and meeting goals, and they experience personal satisfaction as they see community and individual needs addressed and met through their efforts.

For the nursing unit and the university, community-based service learning provides high and positive visibility in the community. The university is viewed by the public as giving back as it shares its information, personnel, and resources.

FUTURE CHALLENGES FOR COMMUNITY-BASED SERVICE LEARNING IN THE NURSING CURRICULUM

Establishing and maintaining a community-based service learning component in the nursing curriculum creates challenges in at least three areas. A major challenge is maintaining the funding needed to provide health screening and education services. A conservative estimate of the cost for only the health screening supplies per semester for the health promotion clinics described in this chapter is $3,000. This amount does not include educational supplies, equipment and equipment maintenance, and office and charting supplies. The vulnerable populations served by the service learning experiences are not required to pay in order to participate, although donations toward supply costs are accepted at the campus clinic. This means that permanent endowments must be found or a series of grants funded in order to continue providing these learning opportunities each semester.

Continuity of services to the community is always a challenge in university settings that function on calendars with extended intercession and summer breaks. Community participants at service learning sites receive health promotion services on a weekly or biweekly basis for a total of only 24 weeks per calendar year if a university is on the semester system and clinical courses are not taught during the summer semester. Although health promotion and self-care are the basis for all community services, participants meet their individual health goals most successfully with the consistent education and encouragement given to them by the students.

A third area of challenge that will always be present in service learning settings is the challenge of balance. How much emphasis should be placed on student learning? What should the balance be between clinical experiences and times for reflection? How much emphasis should be on service to the community? What community needs can be realistically addressed, given time and resources realities? How can the instructor and the administration balance these two competing obligations in a way that has a positive outcome for student learning and for the community's health?

There are no easy answers for maintaining balance or meeting the other challenges of service learning, but the rewards for continuing to offer these experiences are immeasurable. One student spoke for many of his classmates when he wrote, "It changes who you are, if you let it, because the focus is no longer on you. It is on helping others, on serving . . . in a sometimes humble but powerful role."

REFERENCES

American Association of College of Nursing. (1997). *Position statement: A vision of baccalaureate and graduate nursing education*. Washington, DC: Author.

Haight, B., & Burggraf, V. (1992). Reminiscence and life review: Conducting the processes. *Journal of Gerontological Nursing, 18*(2), 39–42.

Hales, A. (1997). Service-learning within the nursing curriculum. *Nurse Educator, 22*(2), 15–18.

Marulio, S. (1996). The service-learning movement in higher education: Academic response to troubled times. *Sociological Imagination, 27*(4), 62, 64–69.

Meyers, S. (1999). Service learning in alternative education settings. *The Clearing House, 73*(2), 114.

Pender, N. (1996). *Health promotion in nursing practice* (3rd ed.). Stamford, CT: Appleton & Lange.

Pew Health Professions Commission. (1995). *Critical challenges: Revitalizing the health professions for the twenty-first century*. San Francisco: UCSF Center for Health Professions.

Serow, R. C., Calleson, D. C., Parker, L. G., & Morgan, L. (1996). Service-learning and the institutional mission of community colleges. *Community College Review, 23*(4), 314.

Sigmon, R. (1979). Service-learning: Three principles. *Synergist, 8*(1), 9–11.

Walker, S. (1996). [Reliabilities for the HPLP-II scale and subscales]. Unpublished raw data.

White, J. L. (1999). Wellness Wednesdays: Health promotion and service learning on campus. *Journal of Nursing Education, 38*(2), 69–71.

CHAPTER

PARISH NURSING: PLANNING FOR COMMUNITY OWNERSHIP

Dr. Helen Sloan

PARISH NURSING—DEFINED AND HISTORY

Parish nursing is a model for delivering care to the whole person in communities of faith to emphasize health promotion and disease prevention (Solari-Twadell, 1999) and is congruent with *Healthy People* 2010 (U.S. Department of Health and Human Services, 2000). This professional nursing practice is developed through seven roles: (1) integrator of faith and health, (2) health educator, (3) personal health counselor, (4) referral agent, (5) trainer of volunteers, (6) developer of support groups and (7) health advocate without an emphasis on the medical model or invasive procedures that encompass the medical model.

Historically, parish nursing was formalized through the work of Granger Westberg, a Lutheran chaplain in the late 1960s (King, Lakin, & Striepe, 1993). He advocated that a group of spiritually oriented family physicians, nurses, and clergy could promote the health of a spiritual community. This successful approach has been adopted in both rural and urban areas by many health care institutions throughout the nation (Solari-Twadell, 1999). The concept of parish nursing may be implemented through four basic organizational models to meet the needs of the faith communities and communities at large. The models range from paid to volunteer, allowing the flexibility that different faith communities need to integrate parish nursing into the life of their congregations. Solari-Twadell (1999) describes these four models as (1) institutional organizational framework, (2) institutional unpaid organizational framework, (3) congregationally paid organizational framework, and (4) congregationally unpaid organizational framework.

COMMUNITY-AS-A-CLIENT LEADS TO PARISH NURSING

Parish nursing is viewed as an important practice of all educational levels of nursing as communities seek improved health care delivery systems (Clemen-Stone, Eigsti, & McGuire, 1995; Hogstel & Diebenow, 1998; Joel, 1998; Magilvy & Brown, 1997; Solari-Twadell, 1999). Parish nursing will provide an ideal setting for students to practice in community settings.

Under the direction of community health nursing faculty, nursing students have learned about the concept of community-as-a-client within a required community health nursing course. The students define a community and assess its core and subsystems. The community assessment wheel (Anderson & McFarlane, 1996) is an excellent standard for students to learn about the community's core (people), economics, recreation, physical environment, education, safety and transportation, politics and government, health and social services, and communication. Students are encouraged to identify the strengths of a community to help develop positive working relationships with communities.

Churches were noted as a strength of the community of Lafayette, Louisiana, during one of these community assessments. Since Lafayette is largely defined by its Cajun culture and catholic heritage, undergraduate student nurses recognized the appropriateness of parish nursing as a community-level intervention in their clinical assignment of Immaculate Heart Community Project in 1995. In collaboration with a local catholic church in a Community Block Development Grant area, these students proposed the role of parish nursing to meet some of the needs of the church's community outreach program. Interest in the concept of parish nursing in the community was evident, although no action derived from this work.

Advanced practice nursing has identified parish nursing as a model for healthier communities (Magilvy & Brown, 1997). A group of graduate students chose to study parish nursing as an advanced nursing intervention for Lafayette and participated in the community committee as described in the following section.

COMMUNITY OWNERSHIP THROUGH CONSULTATION

Nurses in the community health setting have an excellent opportunity to serve as external consultants to assist in determining community health priorities (Anderson & McFarlane, 1996; Stanhope & Alford, 1992). The role of the external consultant includes assessing problems, determining availability and feasibility of resources, proposing solutions, and often assisting with implementation. The community health nurse may serve as a liaison with other community agencies to facilitate processes and to mobilize the skills and knowledge of the whole community.

Collaboration, defined as a process of joint decision making from combined knowledge and skills (Cary, 1992), is integral to the consultant role of the community health nurse. Cary and Androwich (1989) describe six stages of the process of collaboration needed to develop a productive team approach in community health nursing:

- awareness
- tentative exploration and mutual acknowledgement
- trust building
- collegiality
- consensus
- commitment

Using the above model of consultation, relationships with community leaders within Lafayette were developed to promote community ownership of the concept of parish nursing. Graduate and undergraduate nursing students participated in aspects of this collaborative effort.

The concept of parish nursing was discussed with other community leaders, which further validated community interest, and an action initiative was proposed in the healthy communities initiative, A *Vision for Our Future: Partnership for a Healthier Lafayette* (Sloan, 1998). An unofficial committee of persons from various health agencies in Lafayette was organized to foster the development of parish nursing in Lafayette. A consultant attended one committee meeting to share her experiences of developing parish nursing to a defined group of churches in New Orleans.

Graduate nursing students investigated the promotion of parish nursing to improve access to primary health care for communities of faith through fostering partnerships between the health care systems of Lafayette and the community's churches (Gautreau, Smith, & Bringedahl, 1998). Using graduate student input, the unofficial committee decided to plan an educational conference on parish nursing. The students surveyed a large group of churches for interest in the program. Although the mail survey had a low response rate, the committee decided to proceed with planning the educational conference for health care providers and church leaders. Objectives were developed for the conference, and committee members sought resources for the conference.

The unofficial committee had few resources for the conference and decided to partner with The University of Louisiana at Lafayette College of Nursing's Continuing Education department to offer the conference on parish nursing. While this limited the attendance to nurses instead of all health care providers and church members, a beginning education of the community about parish nursing became a reality. Compromise and flexibility is integral to working with a community.

Meanwhile, another member of the health care committee of the healthier communities effort (Sloan, 1998) proposed a parish nursing partnership called The Congregational Wellness Nurse Ministry with a catholic-based medical center. This project (I. Malone, personal communication, April 7, 2000) has been approved by the administration of the medical center and will begin its three-year pilot by targeting populations identified through a community needs assessment. The medical center plans to use a paid model of parish nursing with initial plans of medical center support and congregational support as available. The parish nurses are to meet the standards of parish nursing according to the American Nurses Association (Health Ministries Association, Inc., 1997; Spikes, 1998).

Service learning for nurses and other health professionals may be offered through many approaches. The support for the development of parish nursing in the Lafayette community truly has been an example of consultation and collaboration with various partners for improving health care in the Lafayette community. Ironically, the proposed target for the medical center's pilot parish nursing program is in the subcommunity for which the undergraduate nursing students had identified parish nursing as an intervention. It may not be clearly documented that this resulted from a planned consultative effort; however, it is clear that achieving true community ownership of a community nursing intervention requires that the community define and adapt the intervention to its purpose. Nursing students offer many health-related services to promote healthier communities through their clinical learning experiences with individuals, families, and communities.

REFERENCES

Anderson, E. T., & McFarlane, J. M. (1996). *Community as partner: Theory and practice in nursing* (2nd ed.). Philadelphia: J.B. Lippincott.

Cary, A. (1992). Promoting continuity of care: Advocacy, discharge planning, and case management. In M. Stanhope & J. Lancaster, *Community health nursing: Process and practice for promoting health* (pp. 662–680). St. Louis, MO: Mosby-Year Book.

Cary, A. & Androwich, I. (1989). A collaboration model: A synthesis of literature and research survey. Paper presented at the Association of Community Health Nursing Educators spring institute, Seattle: June, 1989.

Clemen-Stone, S., Eigsti, D. G., & McGuire, S. L. (1995). *Comprehensive community health nursing* (4th ed.). St. Louis, MO: Mosby-Year Book.

Gautreau, R., Smith, W., & Bringedahl, K. (1998). *A community health project: Parish nursing for communities of faith in Lafayette.* Unpublished manuscript, The University of Southwestern Louisiana, Lafayette.

Health Ministries Association, Inc. (1997). *Scope and standards of parish nursing practice.* Unpublished manuscript.

Hogstel, M. O., & Diebenow, K. (1998). Church-based programs. In M. O. Hogstel (Ed.), *Community resources for older adults: A guide for case managers* (pp. 99–122). St. Louis, MO: Mosby-Year Book.

King, J. M., Lakin, J. A., & Striepe, J. (1993). Coalition building between public health nurses and parish nurses. JONA, 23(2), 27–31.

Joel, L. A. (1998). Editorial: Parish nursing: As old as faith communities. *American Journal of Nursing*, 98(8), 7.

Magilvy, J. K., & Brown, N. J. (1997). Parish nursing: Advanced practice nursing model for healthier communities. *Advanced Practice Nursing Quarterly*, 2(4), 67–72.

Sloan, H. (1998). Healthcare action initiatives. *A Vision for Our Future: Partnership for a Healthier Lafayette.* Lafayette, LA: Partnership for a Healthier Lafayette.

Solari-Twadell, P. A. (1999). The emerging practice of parish nursing. In P. A. Solari-Twadell & McDermott, M. A. (Eds.), *Parish nursing: Promoting whole person health with faith communities* (pp. 3–24). Thousand Oaks, CA: Sage.

Solari-Twadell, P. A., & McDermott, M. A. (Eds.). (1999). *Parish nursing: Promoting whole person health with faith communities.* Thousand Oaks, CA: Sage Publications, Inc.

Spikes, J. M. (1998). Standards of parish nurse practice: A presentation at the 5th annual national parish nurse conference. [On-line]. Available: http://www.lcms.org/bhcm/hm/spikes.htm.

Stanhope, M., & Alford, R. (1992). The community health nurse consultant. In M. Stanhope & J. Lancaster, *Community health nursing: Process and practice for promoting health* (pp. 662–680). St. Louis: Mosby-Year Book, Inc.

U.S. Department of Health and Human Services. (2000, January). *Healthy People* 2010 (Conference Edition, in Two Volumes). Washington, DC: Author.

VISITING NURSING FOR HEALTH PROMOTION WITHIN A COLLEGE OF NURSING

Dr. Helen Sloan

VISITING NURSING

Visiting nursing, once called district nursing, is an early mechanism of providing care for families in the home. It was established in 1859 by William Rathbone of Liverpool, England, who had personally seen the value of nursing care in the home and sought to help the poor in his community (Clement-Stone, Eigsti, & McGuire, 1995). He collaborated with Florence Nightingale to found a school to prepare nurses for home visiting. In a similar manner, visiting nursing in the United States developed to serve the poor, primarily in large cities. Buffalo, Boston, and Philadelphia developed visiting nursing during 1885 and 1886. Although visiting nursing in the United States followed no organized development, Lillian Wald promoted the concept of visiting for prevention and family-focused health promotion (Clemen-Stone, Eigsti, & McGuire, 1995). For years, visiting nurse associations (VNAs) and public health departments provided high-quality, low-cost services. The home health industry has now taken over half of the market for nursing care in the home (Fagin, 1986).

Providing care in the community is the preferred option for the elderly who wish to remain in their homes. *Aging in place* is the choice of most citizens of the United States. Even when they need assistance to maintain functional abilities, most elderly wish to stay in their homes rather than be placed in institutions (Cetron, 1987; Nassif, 1987). Meshing support services with housing services is a concept explored by Kane, Illston, Kane, and Nyman (1990) through adult foster care and assisted living. The concept of *aging in place* is the provision of supportive services within a housing complex that does not require movement in that complex. Nurses have been instrumental in advocating and providing for such services.

The increased number of older adults along with the loss of low-cost preventive and health promotion home services through traditional VNAs and public health agencies has left a number of older adults without this needed focus of health care. In addition, families striving to assist their older family members are in need of professional nursing guidance.

Nursing Education Changes

The Pew Health Professions Commission advocated a change in the education of health professionals as the best way to approach the changing vista of health care. The authors have outlined competencies for new practitioners to include a more holistic approach to health care. Health promotion and preventive health care along with efficient, cost-effective care are primary in the list of competencies. The health professional must have the ability to work with the client in his or her world, not just in the clinical aspects of care. The community is expected to be the predominant practice setting for future health care professionals (Huston & Fox, 1998; Shugars, O'Neil, & Bader, 1991).

There is also a curriculum revolution in nursing that encompasses a philosophy of learning instead of training nurses and that provides increased attention to caring for the client rather than only the biomedical aspects of the client (Middlemiss & Neste-Kenny, 1994). Shoultz, Hatcher, and Hurrell state that "... nursing education must return to the practice setting redefined: to teach and learn with our student in those places where people live" (1992, p. 60).

Care of the sick led Lillian Wald to focus on prevention, client education, and the social conditions underlying disease and death. With its present focus on illness, nursing is optimally positioned to lead health care professionals in using the care of the sick in families and communities as a means to engage them in health promotion and disease prevention.

Barnes (1997) offered guidance for gerontological nursing practice in the community. The ultimate goal is to promote a functionally independent life as long as possible through preventive health care and health promotion. It is apparent that the concept of community health nursing today must expand from a focus on maternal-child concerns and communicable diseases to include other populations such as adults and older adults with chronic diseases. This becomes especially important as the care of these persons is shifted to the community.

If the differences in home health care and visiting nurse care are not merged, the nursing profession of inadequately identifying the scope of home health care and is in danger of losing the opportunity to promote wellness and family-centered care (Burbach & Brown, 1988; Reinhard et al., 1996). The qualified home health practitioner must be able to merge the strengths of home visiting with strong clinical skills.

Pavri (1994) challenged nursing students today to share Lillian Wald's vision of a better world as a stimulus to responding to nursing practice of the future. Backer (1993) suggested that Wald's success in transforming values of caring into changing the system of health care to a more humanistic one should continue in today's system.

Wheatley stated that there is a need to stop teaching exclusively factual knowledge and to focus on relationship building as "we give up predictability for potentials" (1992, p. 34). Nursing *tasks* should be replaced with an emphasis on *process*. Building partnerships with individuals, families, and communities to facilitate their quest for health must become the emphasis of nursing process. Reinhard, et al. (1996) suggested that neighborhood nursing may be a method of reconnecting nurses to the communities they serve.

COLLEGE OF NURSING: HOME VISITING FOR HEALTH PROMOTION

Visiting nursing in the College of Nursing at The University of Louisiana at Lafayette has been centered on promoting the health of older adults living at home. This community health nursing experience has allowed a comprehensive clinical experience for students in their senior year, providing opportunities for case management as well as developing partnerships with older adults to promote their health. Families and friends are included if appropriate. Since most older adults live in their homes, this experience is an optimal setting for student nurses working with the aging client. Younger persons may be referred to the program; however, older adults are generally more willing to "be available" to students at the times they are allowed to visit.

Visiting persons in their homes is a vital part of community health nursing at the university. The graduating senior students are assigned clients to follow during their last semester. The purpose of the home visits is to promote the client's health.

The home visiting program is listed as a service to the community in the local Social Service Agency Network's listing of community resources. However, most clients are referred to the home visiting through the various connections of the faculty in the community course. Several agencies in the southwestern Louisiana community serve as referral sites. Among these are the Lafayette Council on Aging, Lafayette senior centers (Greenhouse and Roeehouse), as well as local home health agencies. Apartment complexes for the elderly and handicapped are significant sources of referral. Any agency in the community may refer to the program if its clients meet the criteria for admission to the program.

Eleven "geographical" areas are identified for the visiting nursing experience. Four apartment complexes for older adults and people with disabilities and one duplex housing area comprise the majority of the mini-communities. The apartment complex most recently added is in a nearby small town (approximately 10 miles from the university). Two Community Block Development Grant areas of the city and one church-based referral site are established home visiting areas. The remainder of the sites are identified as geographical portions of the city at large.

PARTNERING WITH COMMUNITY AGENCIES

From the healthier communities efforts of the local community, the faculty recently piloted a Visiting Nurse Initiative called A *Vision for our Future: Partnership for a Healthier Lafayette* (Sloan, 1998). The purpose of this initiative was to formalize a collaborative effort to meet the needs of persons discharged from home health and still needing services that community health nursing students could provide in the home visiting program.

Three faculty met with three of the home health staff to develop content for a letter of agreement between the home health agency and the college of nursing for this semester. Specific criteria for referral were identified, and the following guidelines were established:

- The liaison nurse from the agency would specify discharge status/needs of proposed client(s).
- Faculty from the university college of nursing would previsit prospective client(s) for acceptance into the program.
- Senior students enrolled in community health nursing courses would provide the home visits for health promotion as one aspect of their clinical experiences during the semester.
- Six visits to a client each semester were planned.
- Ongoing consultation with faculty would assure supervision of the student.
- The student and faculty as well as the client would determine continued participation in the program.

Selective services provided by students in home visiting were identified as (1) health education, guidance and counseling; (2) limited procedures such as fingersticks for glucose monitoring; (3) case management; and (4) surveillance. Services *not* provided included treatments, wound care, venipuncture, catherization, IV management, filling Insulin syringes, and taking and carrying out doctors' orders. Clients would be advised to use regular health care during summers and semester breaks.

One client was referred from the partnering hospital-based home health agency the first semester. At the end of the semester, the student wrote a letter to the referring nurse from the home health agency to report the client's status. From the success of this pilot case, two additional clients were followed the next semester, and formalized partnering with additional agencies for this purpose is planned.

PROCESS OF CLIENT INTAKE

Each client accepted into the program is visited by a community health nursing faculty member in order to establish a relationship between the college of nursing and the client. The persons referred are assured that the experience is voluntary and that they may withdraw at any time; however, they are asked to participate for at least one semester (six visits) if at all possible. Faculty orient the client to the purposes of the home visits and leave a large print card with phone numbers so that the client may call the faculty if needed.

During the visits, clients are encouraged to view the student as their "nurse" and the faculty as secondary resources. Visiting the client prior to student assignment provides the faculty with a brief assessment of clients and their environment. Initially, the primary purpose of the visit was to review the area for student safety; however, the brief visit by the faculty has served as reassurance for the client as well. The client (most often an older adult) meets a faculty member in person, has a brief orientation to the purpose of the visits, and is informed of the approximate date of the first visit by the students. Clients are encouraged to ask questions about the program at this time and to share with family and friends that home visits by nursing students will be forthcoming.

CLIENT ORGANIZATION

The senior class size averages 60 students each semester. Clients for these students are organized into geographical areas for several purposes. Students' travel time is reduced by keeping the assignments in a local area, and assignments are facilitated for the faculty by focusing on these mini-communities. The students are organized in the clinical component of the course into eleven small groups, keeping the group size at approximately six persons. Within each group, partners visit each of their clients. Having two visitors helps when family members are present and provides a security measure for students.

STUDENT ORIENTATION AND ASSIGNMENTS

Students are asked to prepare for their first visit by reviewing the chart of their client. Clients' charts are maintained in a double-locked room accessible to the student through a "checked-out" key policy. If the client is new to the program, the student is asked to begin setting up the partnership through obtaining demographic information, including an eco-map and a genogram. During the first visit the student begins to develop rapport with the client. Students may view a video on home visiting or review their text to assist in the process. In addition, an orientation to the home visit is provided by the faculty, which follows the concept of home visiting discussed by Clemen-Stone, Eigsti, & McGuire (1995). The syllabus provides detailed instructions and rules for home visiting, including an emphasis on personal safety.

In subsequent visits the student uses the OMAHA system database guide (Martin & Scheet, 1992) to perform a comprehensive assessment of the client. The faculty member provides guidance to enhance assessments such as mental status, depression, nutrition, and fall prevention. The student and client, together, choose two or three problems that they will focus on during the semester. Students may continue to work on problems identified by students in previous semesters or change as long as the client concurs. For each problem, mutually agreed-upon goals and objectives are developed. The students often use professional contracting as an intervention in promoting achievement of mutually agreed-upon goals and objectives.

Progress in achieving these goals and objectives is documented after every visit. Documentation is through a "visit report" format from the OMAHA system (Martin & Scheet, 1992). At the beginning of the semester, at midpoint, and near the end of the semester the students are asked to rate the outcomes of the work with the OMAHA outcomes rating system. Since the OMAHA system has been automated through the computer software Nightingale Tracker®, which uses the OMAHA system to computerize client records, the faculty have switched to this system through grant support.

Although service learning for graduate programs in nursing is not well documented, Logsdon and Ford (1998) recommend service learning for graduate nursing education. Through a home service learning experience, graduate nursing students are available for limited home visits if the undergraduate student requests the support. This is a recently added experience of the graduate students in the college of nursing at The University of Louisiana at Lafayette.

The visiting nurse program at the university has been operating for more than 10 years. Depending on the number of students, volunteer clients may stay in the program from semester to semester. At the end of the semester and with their client's verbal permission, students recommend continued follow-up for the next semester; however, the faculty make the final decision about retention of clients. Clients may request a semester break but often return to the program.

The success of this program is primarily attributed to its adherence to the service learning philosophy of experiential education based on "reciprocal learning" (Carpenter, 1999). The relationship between the students and their clients is indeed a "win-win" situation. Students have provided positive feedback about their experiences from the beginning, and many ask if they can maintain the relationship after graduation. Individual situations are considered in answering this question. Even those who decide that community health nursing will not be their career focus value the program. When participating in this program, students are confronted with the reality of partnering with clients to promote their health in the world in which they live. Every semester a few students will ask if they can refer clients to the program, and the answer is "yes."

Visiting nursing at the university has been developed around the ethical principle of benevolence (to do good and to do no harm) for both the client and the student. Clients are reassured that the students coming to their home have the preparation needed, and the fact that the students are seniors and near graduation seems to reassure the clients about the student nurses' capabilities. On the other hand, home care, at best, is difficult to monitor and has been criticized as to the quality of home care in general.

The students feel prepared for the independence of this service learning experience since they have several semesters of clinical nursing in more structured settings with faculty at their side. They feel ready for the independent nature of the experience. Although the psychomotor skills are limited without direct faculty supervision, the critical thinking skills are compounded by experiencing the complexity of promoting the health of individuals with various co-morbidities: aging, chronic diseases, and limited resources. Skilled communication is essential in developing a partnership with the client and family as well as in promoting referrals to community resources. Students must fully respect the confidentiality and privacy of clients in the more relaxed home setting.

Faculty actually visit clients before they are accepted into the program. To date, faculty have not had to limit acceptance to the program due to neighborhood safety issues. Students are allowed to visit only on specified days and within specified daytime hours, which seem safer. The faculty have addressed legal and liability issues of home visiting in protecting the students by stressing safety precautions and appropriate student conduct with written policy. This is a critical element of orientation to the experience. As noted by Carpenter and Harrington (1999), the liability of sending students into community settings is a grey area. Preparing the student as well as the client for the experience has served as a positive aspect of this service learning program.

REFERENCES

Backer, B. A. (1993). Lillian Wald: Connecting caring with activism. *Nursing & health care*, 14(3), 122–129.

Barnes, S. J. (1997). Gerontological care in community care settings. In M. A. Matteson, E. S. Mcconnell, & A. D. Linton, *Gerontological nursing: Concepts and Practice* (2nd ed, pp. 897–929). Philadephia, PA: W.B. Saunders Co.

Burbach, C. A., & Brown, B. E. (1988). Community health and home health nursing: Keeping the concepts clear. *Nursing & health care*, 9(2), 97–100.

Carpenter, D. R. (1999). The concept of service-learning. In P. A. Bailey, D. R. Carpenter, & P. A. Harrington, (Eds.), *Integrating community service into nursing education: A guide to service-learning* (pp. 1–18). New York: Springer.

Carpenter, D. R., & Harrington, P. (1999). The promises and problems of service-learning. In P. A. Bailey, D. R. Carpenter, & P. A. Harrington (Eds.), *Integrating community service into nursing education: A guide to service-learning* (pp. 65–78). New York: Springer.

Cetron, M. (1987). Public opinion of home health care. *Generations*, 11(2), 42–44.

Clemen-Stone, S., Eigsti, D. G., & Mcguire, S. L. (1995). *Comprehensive community health nursing: Family, aggregate, & community practice* (4th ed.). St. Louis, MO: Mosby.

Fagin, C. M. (1986). Opening the door on nursing's cost advantage. *Nursing and Health Care*, 7(7), 352–357.

Huston, C. J., & Fox, S. (1998). The changing health care market: Implications for nursing education in the coming decade. *Nursing Outlook*, 46, 109–14.

Kane, R. A., Illston, L. H., Kane, R. L. & Nyman, J. A. (1990). *Meshing services with housing: Lessons from adult foster care and assisted living in Oregon*. Minneapolis, MN: University of Minnesota, Long-Term Care DECISIONS Resource Center.

Logsdon, M. C., & Ford, D. (1998). Service learning for graduate students. *Nurse Educator*, 23(2), 34–37.

Martín, K., & Scheet, N. J. (1992). *The Omaha system: Applications for community health nursing*. Philadelphia: W.B. Saunders.

Middlemiss, M. A., & Neste-Kenny, J. V. (1994). Curriculum revolution: Reflective minds and empowering relationships. *Nursing & health care*, 15(7), 350–353.

Nassif, J. Z. (1987). There's still no place like home. *Generations*, 11(2), 5–8.

Pavri, J. M. (1994). Overview one hundred years of public health nursing: Visions of a better world. *Imprint*, 41(4), 43, 45, 47–48.

Reinhard, S. C., Christopher, M. A., Mason, D. J., McConnell, K., Rusca, P., & Toughill, E. (1996). Promoting health communities through neighborhood nursing. *Nursing Outlook*, 44(5), 223–228.

Shoultz, J., Hatcher, P. A., & Hurrell, M. (1992). Growing edges of a new paradigm: The future of nursing in the health of the nation. *Nursing Outlook*, 40(2), 57–61.

Shugars, D. A., O'Neil, E. H., & Bader, J. D. (Eds.). (1991). *Healthy America: Practitioners for 2005, an agenda for action for U.S. health professional schools*. Durham, NC: The Pew Health Professions Commission.

Sloan, H. (1998). Healthcare action initiatives. A *Vision for our Future: Partnership for a Healthier Lafayette*. Lafayette, LA: Partnership for a Healthier Lafayette.

Wheatley, M. J. (1992). *Leadership and the new science: Learning about organization from an orderly universe*. San Francisco: Berrett-Koehler.

SERVICE LEARNING IN A MIGRANT FARM WORKERS' CLINIC

Sara C. Majors
Carolyn White
Pamela Martin
John P. McGuinnes

Service learning is a unique approach to health care education, which combines the educational process with community service. As this link is forged, a synergy results in which the learner's knowledge expands simultaneously with community engagement and service. Service learning is a form of experiential education in which students utilize previous knowledge to address community needs. Through service learning, the application of critical thinking in structured opportunities offers students of various health disciplines an innovative learning experience. The students are exposed to cultural diversity and through community service develop values that emphasize respect for fellow man (Zlotkowski, 2000). Service learning in the health care setting incorporates social justice in the delivery of health care and the empowerment of underserved populations. The purpose of this chapter is to describe an actual service learning project in Alabama where an interdisciplinary team of health providers "teach through service" with remarkable results. The application of the principles of service learning as applied in the design and implementation of the project will be fully explored in the following scenario.

Rosa Hernandez comes through the doors of the Baldwin County Health Department in Robertsdale, Alabama late on a summer afternoon. It has already been a long day for Rosa working at a local commercial nursery lifting and bending hundreds of times to transplant house plants, but compared to life in her native village in Mexico, transplanting houseplants is not a bad life. Rosa hates missing work for any reason; she knows all too well that missing work means missing pay. It was difficult getting to the clinic; there are no buses in the remote part of the county where she resides. Since she does not have a car, Rosa must rely on acquaintances for a ride, and, of course, they expect to be paid. Rosa already has two daughters, ages two and three, and she thinks she is pregnant again. Rosa has no insurance. Most of her cash resources are used for her daily needs. What little remains is sent home to her extended family in Mexico.

Rosa has heard that this clinic will provide free medical care to migrant workers. Rosa is particularly worried about her pregnancy. Her friends have told her that local doctors are expensive and must be paid before the baby is born. There are numerous papers to be signed, and they are all written in English. She has had three pregnancies, and one of her pregnancies ended in the premature birth of her baby, much too young to survive in rural Mexico. She prays that this will not happen again.

The clinic waiting room is full of people, many of whom appear to be Hispanic. From the front desk a well-dressed lady, obviously not a farm worker, greets Rosa in fluent Spanish and asks her to sign a waiting list. The woman has a friendly manner and speaks Mexican Spanish. A poster in the waiting room explains that children need immunizations for protection. The poster is in Spanish!

Eventually Rosa is called to an examining room where two students take her blood pressure; an older woman in a long white coat enters, speaks to the two, then takes the blood pressure herself as the two students observe.

Rosa's encounter with the clinic did not just happen, but rather occurred as a result of the process that began with an effort to define the needs of the migrant workers population in the county. Prior to establishing the Clinica del Migrante, Inc., a group of health care practitioners conducted a community assessment regarding barriers to health care for migrant workers. Collaboration with the migrant workers via churches, employers, and schools gained the first-person perspective of the difficulties faced. As the surveys were conducted, a number of recurring themes emerged. The migrant workers have a great deal of difficulty in locating Spanish speaking clinicians. Further, operating hours of most doctors' offices are not compatible with their work schedules and the workers are reluctant to miss work time for a doctor's appointment. The expense of obtaining medical care creates a major barrier. Most of the income of migrant workers goes to pay for food and housing. Like other underinsured and uninsured, they cannot afford the prepayment required by many practitioners or the expense of periodic visits to the hospital emergency department (Garcia de Pasada, 1999). Prenatal care is a special need for most migrant workers. The care is both essential and expensive, elements that create health crises for the families as well as the local community. The majority of migrant farm workers receive care either from health departments or local providers on an urgent basis only or not at all. By virtue of their employment and culture, migrant farm workers have specific health care needs and face multiple barriers to basic health care services (Migrant Clinicians Network, 1997).

As the largest county and leading crop producer in Alabama, Baldwin County has a large number of migrant and seasonal farm workers. The total labor bill for migrant farm workers in Baldwin County in 1992 was nearly one million dollars (Census of Agriculture, 1992). This is the highest figure for any Alabama county, implying the large numbers of migrant workers employed in this county compared to the rest of the state. Over the last few years the number of migrant workers in the area has grown dramatically, and the local health care community has increasingly recognized the needs of the migrant workers. There have been a number of well-intentioned programs for the migrant workers, but no comprehensive primary care site has been established. In addition, the health care community has been aware of the needs of the uninsured population. The working poor are numerous, typically earning too much income to qualify for Medicaid or too little to purchase conventional health insurance. The local health department has tried to cope with the needs of the underserved population, but due to declining funding and lack of practitioners, it has been unable to satisfy basic health care needs.

The College of Nursing and the Department of Physical Therapy of the University of South Alabama supports increased diversity in their training sites. In addition, as the concept of the nurse practitioner has evolved and has become popularized, the college has, by necessity, sought new training sites. Similarly, the Department of Physical Therapy has required new sites for clinical experiences to supplement the decreased availability of local physical therapy clinic/training sites. Culturally diverse sites offer an excellent medium to implement a health promotion model of primary care (Martin & Fell, 1999).

The two student nurses interviewed Ms. Hernandez with the help of a volunteer translator. They also spent a few minutes reviewing the importance of abstaining from alcohol, tobacco, and drugs while pregnant. It was obvious that the students enjoyed applying the knowledge they had learned in the classroom to a real patient. Even though the students lived locally and had not traveled very far, they did not realize that non-English speaking people in Alabama were experiencing so many barriers to care. Their experience in the clinic opened their eyes to the changes that were taking place in America.

Later that day the nursing students who had cared for Rosa gathered with the other learners in the clinic break room for a formal discussion of the day's activities. The students talked about what they had learned and how Rosa's dedication to her children and job had impressed them. One of the other learners commented that his experience in the clinic has altered his perception of "illegal aliens" coming to the United States for "welfare." He was starting to see that people like Rosa were essential to the local agricultural economy, and rather than looking for welfare, migrant workers worked hard for relatively low wages to provide for their families. He was now realizing that there were hard-working people in the community who did not have access to the basic health care that most people take for granted. The students realized that if not for the nurse practitioners, doctor, and physical therapist at the clinic, people like Rosa and her children would not receive any health care. They now understood that only a small portion of the nation's health care workforce administers care to migrant workers. They were impressed to learn that most of the health care for migrant workers is delivered by nurse practitioners (Sandhaus, 1998).

The active participation of the learners in positions of responsibility is a key component of service learning. Though the nursing students were unaware, they were engaged in a service learning program. By helping to meet Rosa's need for health care, they were serving the common good of the community. The students learned the proper technique of blood pressure measurement and the importance of the accurate recording of Rosa's vital signs. They also educated Rosa about the risks of alcohol, tobacco, and drugs in pregnancy. The service learning opportunity at the clinic includes discussions for all learners about their experiences with the patients. These discussions should not be limited to clinical or academic issues but should include relevant social justice issues, such as access to health care for the uninsured and the exploration of attitudes toward immigrants in our society, especially those with a different language and culture. Exploring the impact of cultural beliefs on the patients' health problems should be included in student discussions (Bechtel, 1995). This reflective component of service learning is important in placing the entire educational experience in perspective. Further, it emphasizes the premise that a well-rounded education incorporates moral lessons with mastery of facts.

Due to the combination of poverty, limited access to health care, and hazardous working conditions, migrant farm workers suffer mortality and morbidity rates greater than the majority of the American population. Second only to mining, farm work is the most dangerous occupation in the United States. Consequently, the average life span of the migrant worker is estimated at 49 years of age compared to 74 years of age for most Anglo-Americans (Migrant Clinicians Network, 1997). Some health concerns are clearly attributable to the occupational hazards of farm work. Dermatitis and respiratory problems caused by natural fungi, dust, and pesticide exposures are common. Lack of safe drinking water contributes to dehydration and heat stroke. The absence of toilet facilities leads to urinary retention, increasing the risk of urinary tract infection (National Center for Farmworker Health, 1990).

In most Latino cultures, a present time orientation is embraced, which influences health behaviors. Since most migrant farm workers are Latino, treatment for chronic conditions is often not a priority (Slesinger, 1992). Conditions such as tuberculosis, diabetes, cancer, and HIV, which require careful monitoring and frequent treatment, pose special problems for farm workers who must move frequently. As a predominantly Hispanic population, farm workers are particularly vulnerable to diabetes and its consequences.

Migrant farm workers have a high rate of chronic diarrhea. Up to 78% of all migrant farm workers suffer from parasitic infection compared to 2% or 3% of the general population. Farm workers suffer from the highest rate of toxic chemical injuries of any group of workers in the United States. More than any other working group, farm workers suffer and die from heat stress and dehydration. Many of the illnesses that migrant farm workers suffer from are vaccine preventable, and the majority of preschool-age farm worker children are not appropriately vaccinated for their age level. The death rates for farm workers from influenza and pneumonia have been reported to be as much as 20% and 200% higher, respectively, than the national average (Sweeney and Ciesielski, 1990).

In another part of the clinic, a preceptor reviews an earlier patient encounter with a new nurse practitioner student. Such discussions between learner and preceptor are a regular part of the educational program at the clinic. It was the student's first experience with a "real" patient other than in the setting of a traditional med-surg unit, and he was obviously nervous. The preceptor had monitored the entire encounter and wanted the student to know he had done a good job for a beginner. As a preceptor, she knew that her supervision was important to the student's professional development. She used these evaluations to help the learner attain his learning goals. An observer of the preceptor-student interaction would have noted the bidirectional nature of the communication. It was obvious that the learner benefited from the preceptor's insights and that the preceptor would use the learner's comments in her evaluation of other learners.

The key features of the learning component of a service learning program include training, supervision, and monitoring of the learner (Zlotkowski, 2000). All participants benefit from the service learning program at Clinica del Migrante. The nursing students embrace social issues and learn basic assessment skills while mastering the technique of blood pressure measurement. The client is educated about the importance of prenatal care. The students receive timely and constructive feedback from the preceptor and are mentored throughout the process. Communication in the program is multidirectional.

Down the hall, a physical therapy student was beginning a postural and body mechanics evaluation of another pregnant patient. Under supervision, the student observed the patient standing and lifting objects of varying size and weight and gave instructions to the patient on correct posture and good body mechanics.

Through the interpreter, the student also taught exercises and relaxation techniques and addressed other issues sometimes associated with pregnancy, such as pelvic floor impairments, carpal tunnel syndrome, low back and sacro-iliac joint discomfort, correction of Diastasis Recti, and varicose veins. During this time the student noticed several things. Firstly, seeing a patient who speaks another language resulted in a longer treatment session because everything was spoken twice—once by either the therapist or patient and once by the interpreter. Second, the student realized that she was having to think ahead, plan, and prioritize her statements to the patient. Clear and concise communication was required to adequately communicate with the patient. Further, the student realized that what she learned in her patient education class was true; that is, many factors such as socioeconomic status, literacy level, language, and cultural barriers play a large role in the communication and trust between the physical therapist and the patient. Finally, unlike many of her other clinical affiliations, here at the migrant clinic the physical therapy student was able to see and treat the patient as a "whole" patient and not just "a knee" or "a back."

Like the students in other disciplines, the physical therapy student is engaged in a service learning program. The student is given an opportunity to put into practice the knowledge and skills she has previously learned in the classroom through the evaluation and treatment of the migrant clients. Being coached along the way by clinical faculty, this student is being prepared for future practice in underserved areas (White, 1999).

The clients in the clinic waiting area were not all Mexican or Spanish speaking. An African-American man wanted to be seen for a rash on his feet. He worked at a fish-processing shed but had no insurance. He had been to the clinic before for a number of problems and knew he would be treated with respect and compassion although he couldn't pay. He was born and raised in the county and has eyed the influx of Spanish speaking farm workers with a bit of suspicion. But as he sat in the clinic, he realized that these people were not much different from himself. A White woman with two small children with runny noses got his attention. She was a single parent, between jobs, and without any money for an office visit. She liked the fact that both she and her children could be seen here and, at the last visit, her children watched a video about brushing their teeth and were given toothbrushes. Since then it's been much easier getting them to brush. She commented to him how nice these people are to her.

The clinic is established to remove some of the barriers that prevent access to health care for migrant farm workers and poor, uninsured people in the local community. Like many other institutions in the American South, the clinic is sensitive to the region's history of racial and economic discrimination and provides a remedy. That the clinic services are made available to all regardless of race, gender, language, immigration status, and/or sexual orientation is apparent from its opening day. What is less obvious is that the clinic seeks to maintain an equally diverse staff. Among them, too, there is a genuine atmosphere in the clinic that anyone who participates as either a learner, provider, or patient brings something to be exchanged for either knowledge or aid. Service learning programs promote participation by diverse populations, and each program has a deep-seated commitment to the elimination of barriers to participation by learners and patients.

Service learning in the health care setting has unique components not always found in other community-based training. Social justice is a necessary ingredient of the service learning program at Clinica del Migrante. Health care professionals are able to provide a benefit to the community they serve, but in serving a medically underserved community, they deliver social justice as well. As the students learn, they provide critical service to their patients and offer validation to the notion that no matter how humble the occupation of a person, one is entitled to health care delivered in a compassionate and timely manner.

A necessary ingredient for service learning in a health care training program is the empowerment of not only the learners but also the clients. It is apparent from the scenarios described that the learners are developing the technical and interpersonal skills essential to their profession while empowering the patients. Ms. Hernandez is learning that she is responsible for the well-being of her unborn child and that she can influence the outcome of her pregnancy by abstaining from alcohol and tobacco. Similarly, the African-American man, the single mother, and her children all benefit from visiting the clinic. The man is able to continue working, and the single mother sees her role as a mother strengthened through the knowledge that she is helping to preserve her children's dental health.

The clinic did not simply materialize as a result of good intentions but rather resulted from a carefully charted course laid out by concerned people. The establishment of a community-based medical clinic for migrant workers and other community members required the coordination of local governmental agencies such as the health department, a local academic institution, a local pharmacy, and churches into a functioning health care network. Numerous meetings were required to define the role of each organization. Each individual player in the network shared in the network's vision of the importance of unencumbered access to health care for migrant workers and other uninsured populations.

The overall responsibility for the management of the clinic rested with a board of directors drawn from the local community, the volunteer pool, and the target population as well. The board was charged with insuring that the clinic maintained its commitment to health care for the underserved and that the clinic's management applied sound fiscal principles.

To become an effective service learning organization, the clinic defined the responsibilities of each community agency and individual involved in the network. Defining these required a series of careful negotiations directed at resolving issues surrounding task identification, timing, and philosophical issues. The preparation was completed within the context of providing for the health care needs of the underserved. The parties in the network understood that their responsibilities and the services offered by the clinic could change as the needs of the target population changed. Today, the clinic is a dynamic entity demonstrating responsiveness to the needs of both the learners and the community.

The clinic staff knew that to have a prolonged and beneficial effect on their community they would need sustained and active commitment from the College of Nursing, the Department of Physical Therapy, and the local community. They had worked in concert with the college to provide not only a clinical site but also a fertile field for health care research; a number of faculty members authored peer-reviewed publications and presented at local, state, and regional levels as a result of their work at the clinic. The clinic actively sought to maintain its connection to the local community by developing a speakers program. Staff members would provide a slide program at the request of any organization. The speaker emphasizes not only the clinic's efforts to serve the community but also the contributions made to the clinic by the community organizations (including volunteers, funds, and supplies) as well as the ongoing need for funding.

A strong service learning program has deep roots in the community, the sponsoring organizations, and the population it serves. Clinica del Migrante fosters a strong link to the curricula at the College of Nursing and the College of Allied Health. The connection between the need for cultural diversity and clinical rotation results in a strong response among several health disciplines. A steady stream of students seeking opportunities within underserved populations has been witnessed. Because of the ongoing need for funding, skills such as grant writing are taught, which provides graduate students unique opportunities to impact real people with real needs. Similarly, communication, collaboration, and leadership skills are recognized and are put to use quickly. Because of the interdisciplinary nature of the training at Clinica del Migrante, respect, interdependence, and teamwork emerge with seeming spontaneity.

Through the medium of dire need, graphic illustrations of the significance of intervention are realized. Such messages are not best taught in the classroom but in communities where people live. Outpatient, community-based sites provide distinct opportunities for learning. Cultural sensitivity, leadership, assessment savvy, communication, and collaboration skills are only some of the expected outcomes. Deep personal satisfaction, the emergence of a sense of professional mission, purpose, and commitment are a few of the unexpected yet not uncommon gains. Service in the community allows academia to demonstrate partnership in training via local advocacy. Tomorrow's best health provider will be technically and humanistically balanced and will be capable of adapting to a variety of health care settings both within and outside the hospital in rural and urban areas. Service learning allows the best opportunity to discover such potential. Its use can transform communities and universities and can shape the health care leader of tomorrow.

REFERENCES

Bechtel, G. A., Shepherd, M. A., et al. (1995). Family, culture, and health practices among immigrant farm workers, *Journal of Community Health Nursing*, Issue 12(1): 15–22.

Census of Agriculture. (1992). *Total labor bill CROP labor expenses Alabama*. Migrant Clinicians Network. (1997). Available: *http://www.nass.usda.gov/census/census92/volume1/al-1/92al.htm*

Garcia de Pasada, R. (1999). *Expanding private health coverage to uninsured Hispanic Americans*. Washington DC: The Heritage Foundation.

Martin, P., & Fell, D. (1999). Beyond treatment: Patient education for health promotion and disease prevention. *Journal of Physical Therapy Education*, 13(3).

National Safety Council. (April, 1990). Accident Facts. Available: http://www.ncfh.org/aboutfws/basic.htm.

Sandhaus, S. (1998). Migrant health: A harvest of poverty. *American Journal of Nursing*, 98(9), 52–54.

Slesinger, D. P. (1992). Health status and needs of migrant farm workers in the United States: A literature review. *Journal of Rural Health*, 8(3), 227–34.

White, C. (1999, Winter). Developing a minority sensitive nurse mentoring program. *Minority Nurse*. September; 51–53.

Zlotkowski, E. (2000, February 25). Handout presented at lecture at University of South Alabama College of Nursing, Mobile, AL.

THE COMMUNITY HEALTH RESOURCE FAIR AS A SERVICE LEARNING TOOL

Jill Laroussini

A service learning activity, the Community Health Resource Fair (CHRF), was designed to orient baccalaureate nursing students to area community resources. The CHRF hosts representatives of social service agencies at a central location on campus in order to generate an experience for each nursing student to meet and interface with agency representatives. The CHRF promotes student learning and furthers professional development with an expanded awareness of agencies in the area and the services they provide. This experience also gives students insight into population needs, community problems, and current solutions offered within the community where they will begin their nursing practice as students under faculty direction. Each of these agencies may be useful as a referral resource in the management of client care throughout the students' education and future practice.

The CHRF is a unique curricular application that is congruent with Jacoby's (1996) description of service learning as "experiential education . . . where students engage in activities that address human and community needs together with structured opportunities intentionally designed to promote student learning and development" (p. 8). Student learning at the CHRF is structured by assigning faculty-written case scenarios for students to problem solve utilizing the referral agencies that they learn about at the fair. Descriptions of the inception and evolution of a CHRF and the outcomes at one department of nursing are presented in this chapter.

THE INCEPTION OF A COMMUNITY HEALTH RESOURCE FAIR

During the last semester of clinical course work, senior nursing students at UL Lafayette are required to make home-based visits to older adults for health promotion and case management as well as function in case management roles in

other community-based sites. The orientation to area resources originally consisted of having three guest speakers from their respective social service agencies address the students in one afternoon at the beginning of the semester. With
such a limited orientation, the students often sought faculty guidance to learn
about referral resources that were appropriate for home-based clients. At the end
of the 12-week clinical period, students reported that they were much better prepared yet expressed a wish to have had better knowledge of community resources from the beginning. Orienting students to only three agencies did not
provide an ideal preparation for the clinical experiences ahead, and adding more
agencies to the agenda was not a sensible solution given the time constraints. In
brainstorming a way to introduce the students to more than three community resources (preferably in a more interactive fashion than a guest speaker/lecture format) without dedicating considerably more time, community health faculty members derived the idea of a fair that would bring the many resources to campus for
an event to be called the Community Health Resource Fair (CHRF). This fair
would serve the need to orient the nursing students to the multitude of social
service agencies and the various types of services they provide and it also would
benefit the agencies by helping them to reach more people and get their message out. Many of these agencies are small, nonprofit agencies with one or two
paid staff members and a host of volunteers to carry out their mission. Participation in this fair essentially allowed the agencies to extend case-finding efforts to
the population they serve by educating two hundred clinical nursing students
that were due to be placed in a variety of community-based sites.

The idea of a CHRF was presented to the curriculum committee. The nursing
faculty recognized the value of this type of orientation for their students, as all
of the courses with clinical components included at least one community-based
clinical learning site. An ad hoc committee of four faculty members, each representing a different clinical course across all levels of the curriculum, was formed
to develop the assignments that would provide structure for the students as
they visited each social service agency at the fair. The assignments included a
case scenario that described a problem similar to the type of clinical problems
anticipated in their specific clinical areas. Students were to problem solve the
scenarios individually or in small groups with a holistic view. Students were instructed to not only address the problem identified in the hypothetical situation described but also to be creative and anticipate risk factors and other
needs. For instance, students were expected to anticipate caregiver burden for
the wife of the elderly client with advanced dementia and to consider all referrals available—from respite care to assistance with housekeeping and shopping
needs—in order to support the caregiver in caring for the client.

THE FIRST CHRF

The original planning of the first CHRF was initiated in the fall semester by one
faculty member who was assisted by eight students. The students earned
class credit for their role in planning the fair. The students read a recent needs

assessment conducted by two area hospitals and were assigned one of the following focus areas to investigate: Abuse and Neglect, Aging/Elderly, Alcohol/Drug Abuse Prevention and Treatment, Basic and Emergency Services, Employment, Family Support, Health and Rehabilitation, and Youth Services. A list of agencies representing each focus area was also provided. Students researched current issues related to the focus area and learned about the agency services and eligibility criteria. A prioritized list of agencies to invite to the fair was submitted for each focus area. Upon faculty approval, the students made phone calls to invite the agency representatives to attend the fair. The faculty member followed up by mailing an invitation with an RSVP form. Forty-four agencies accepted the invitation, and the first CHRF was held in the third week of the spring semester.

The planning is now conducted by a committee of five faculty who periodically collect new agency names for inclusion in the fair. The committee is assisted by one departmental secretary to print and mail invitations to agency participants. The committee chairperson collects RSVPs, designs the floor plan for the fair, and coordinates planning with the location (ballroom) personnel. Committee members design evaluation tools, coordinate with campus catering for refreshments, disseminate information about the fair to other faculty, and further develop the case scenarios used to structure student learning.

The case scenarios written by clinical faculty closely resemble the types of patient situations that students will encounter in the clinical area. There are two basic types of questions in the scenarios. The first type, used by all clinical faculty, is a comprehensive description of a client's illness/injury and the parameters that the nurse would assess for the discharge-planning process: who the primary caregivers are, how they will pay for home care, what entitlements they are eligible for, and what the care needs at home will be. This comprehensive case description is followed by questions that direct the student to identify which agencies represent appropriate referrals. The other type of question is termed 'a scavenger hunt'-type question. A simple, straightforward question beginning with "where would you find . . ." or "who can provide . . ." directs the student to locate an agency that provides a specific service.

The senior students focusing on community mental health will require knowledge of many referral resources to function in the case management roles so their scenarios consist of one comprehensive description and several 'scavenger hunt'-type questions. This structures the learning such that senior students must seek referral resources for clients in all age ranges, from infancy to elderly. One such scenario designed for senior students is as follows:

You are a community nurse assigned to work with residents of several HUD housing units. One of your assigned units is primarily made up of young mothers and school-age children. There are also many preschoolers, toddlers, and infants. What are some of the community agencies you anticipate collaborating with and what services do they provide? What are the eligibility criteria and costs of these services?

After several months of assessment and coming to know this community, you learn of several residents that have chronic mental illnesses. What additional agencies are available to meet the needs of this population?

Scavenger Hunt Questions:

What support services are available for deaf persons in our area?

Who qualifies for the 'Meals on Wheels' Program by the Council on Aging?

How can you get a wheelchair ramp built when you cannot pay a carpenter?

The case scenarios are provided to the students in writing on the morning of the fair with instructions to "problem solve the following scenario by using the resources you learn about at the Community Health Resource Fair." Students are encouraged to be creative and are not restricted to using only those agencies that are presently in attendance.

No fees are required of agency participants for table space at the fair. Many agencies are government funded or small, nonprofit agencies and could not afford the expense of a table fee. The expenses involved in producing the fair are minimal. Postage for the invitations was absorbed by the departmental mailing budget. The refreshments, which consist of a light lunch (sandwiches, fruit and vegetable tray, cookies, punch, and coffee), are paid out of departmental funds and cost less than $300.

THE DAY OF THE CHRF

The CHRF is held on a clinical day from 9:00 A.M. to 3:00 P.M. at the Student Union Ballroom located centrally on campus. Agency participants arrive one hour before the doors open and begin to set up displays. The committee chairperson accompanied by one additional faculty from the committee and two or three student volunteers are present to greet the agency participants and to guide them to their tables. A hand truck is kept in the reception area, and student volunteers assist in transporting heavy boxes of brochures to agency tables. Coffee is offered to agency participants in the morning, and a light lunch is offered near the noon hour. Arrival times are assigned for each class to better control the traffic flow of people attending the CHRF at one given time.

Upon arrival students walk from table to table to view the posters and displays of each agency. They take the brochures for future reference and interface with the agency representatives, asking questions in attempts to solve the problems presented in their assigned case scenario. Course faculty often attend with their class and are available to guide the students if needed. Students learn about volunteer opportunities, referral resources for clients and family members, and the vast variety of services available to support needs in the community. Students encounter services for needs that they may have never encountered, including homelessness and domestic violence.

Students may work in groups, pairs, and individually to learn of resources to solve problems presented in the scenarios. Upon completion of the scenarios, the students return to class and present the information discovered for shared learning. Faculty have observed the students express enthusiasm during the shared learning presentations about discovering agencies that will actually help clients and families with real needs.

AGENCY FEEDBACK

Agency participants are pleased to be able to offer solutions to the problems in the scenarios and frequently offer ideas for additional scenarios that match services they offer. Evaluations collected at the end of the fair document that they enjoyed the challenging questions and the complexity of the case scenarios. Agency participants have frequently acknowledged the compassion with which the students proceed in seeking resources to match the needs of families described in the case scenarios.

Agency participants have also provided feedback on constructing scenarios that compliment the services that they offer. The first year that Red Cross participated, the representative requested inclusion of a scenario about a family who had lost all possessions to a house fire. Additional reported benefits are the opportunities to recruit new volunteers and to learn of new agencies and the newly added services of existing ones while networking with the other representatives. Many of the social service agencies overlap in areas of interest and serve the same client population. This service learning fair provides another networking opportunity to initiate new or to further develop collaboration among groups with a common mission.

FACULTY FEEDBACK

Faculty in attendance at the CHRF were able to update existing knowledge of area resources and network with agency participants to collaboratively meet client and classroom teaching needs. Alliances made with the newly formed Hepatitis C support group helped one faculty member to secure a guest lecturer and lecture material to enhance the presentation of theory content regarding diseases of the liver. Another faculty member collaborated with agency personnel to identify a future clinical site in the community. Faculty reported positively on the creative process that students used to problem solve scenarios and observed a subsequent increase in confidence among students functioning in the discharge-planning roles in the inpatient clinical sites. Additionally, students who were not yet formally introduced to discharge-planning concepts were observed initiating referrals with family members on behalf of their clients. Overall, faculty are very positive about the CHRF and the resultant impact on student learning.

STUDENT FEEDBACK

Students report increased knowledge of area social service agencies and an expanded awareness of the types of social problems in the community. They enjoy the creative group process and shared learning in the classroom. Their toolbox of assessment skills has been expanded by a now familiar list of referral sources to match client needs. Having attended the fair and having considered several scenarios in the classroom, students in the inpatient settings can better anticipate post-discharge needs and are better prepared to assist with appropriate referrals to meet those needs. Students report an increased confidence in being able to help others. It may actually be that they are either better able or perhaps more willing to distinguish certain needs when they know of resources that provide a solution to that need. Another noted outcome of the interactions with agency participants is that of an increase in volunteering as students find out about agency needs that match their interests and capabilities.

Students begin the orientation to the semester with an introduction to service learning concepts. The activity of attending the CHRF provides the students with tools that consist of knowledge of area referral resources that help them to creatively address hypothetical situations that they are likely to encounter in the clinical setting. Reflection about the scenarios and realistic solutions are shared in the classroom. This structured learning is designed to enhance service learning values, to foster development of the student, and to build their knowledge base of familiar resources that will ultimately serve the client population and the community. The activity is experiential, and students will soon have an opportunity to apply this knowledge in the development of their nursing practice in every future clinical setting. The CHRF has proven to be a win-win, service learning activity for all involved and continues to grow and expand possibilities for all involved.

REFERENCE

Jacoby, B. (1996). *Service learning in higher education: Concepts and practices.* San Francisco: Jossey-Bass.

CHAPTER

CONTINUING EDUCATION: A LIFELONG SERVICE LEARNING CONCEPT

Belinda Poor

The College of Nursing and Allied Health Professions continuing education program at UL Lafayette was established in December of 1981 in response to a request from the professional nurses in the community. The program provides a variety of educational offerings, including clinical nursing programs, faculty development programs, and programs cosponsored through contractual arrangements with area health care agencies and organizations.

The continuing education program is based on the belief that the completion of basic and advanced programs in nursing provides an initial foundation for continued learning throughout a lifetime of practice. This program recognizes that nurses practice in diverse settings with clients across the lifespan and across the continuum. Knowledge updates in the areas of health promotion and disease prevention are as critical to improvement in the health status of the community as updates in acute care technology and practice. Nurses share with other health professionals the challenges of a rapid expansion in knowledge and technology and an increased pace of societal change that requires this philosophy of lifelong learning. When appropriate, multidisciplinary collaboration in the development of continuing education offerings encourages a sharing of knowledge among health professionals.

To determine and meet the educational needs of the learners, an assessment of needs is done on a regular basis. Since end of life issues are usually a priority, the continuing education program planned a regional conference on end of life issues.

This conference began as a nursing conference but developed into a multidisciplinary conference. One of the goals of the continuing education program is to provide programs with a multidisciplinary focus to promote collaboration with other health care providers for the purpose of improving health care. A multidisciplinary team was developed, which consisted of registered nurses, educators, social workers, grief counselors, and physicians.

This team identified educational needs and began to plan a regional conference for health care providers who are faced with end of life issues in their practice. In the process, the team recognized that, in general, people in the community were not fully aware of end of life issues that they may encounter. The decision was then made to add a public forum entitled "Mapping The Way Through The End of Life."

Since this additional forum was developed for the general public community, many disciplines were involved. It was suggested that senior nursing students enrolled in the community nursing course could benefit by participating in planning this forum. The assignment, in general, would require students to identify all disciplines and/or community resources involved in end of life care. These students would then plan a forum presentation by some of the leaders identifying what disciplines or community resources are available to the public, such as social security officers, insurance representatives, funeral directors, financial planners, attorneys, bereavement counseling providers, financial assistance, hospice programs, and so on. These community resources would be invited to present information concerning their particular services to the public at the end of life forum. The students would be responsible for developing a "map" of how to access these resources and would direct the participants to the correct community resource that could provide the information they needed. Participants would then be able to attain information that would answer their questions concerning end of life issues.

In planning this program, the following three principles of service learning defined by Sigmon (1979, p. 10), a leader in service as a tool for learning, were identified:

1. Those being served control the service(s) provided.
2. Those being served become better able to serve and be served by their own actions.
3. Those who serve are also learners and have significant control over what is expected to be learned.

SERVICE LEARNING PRINCIPLE ONE: PARTICIPANT CONTROL

The first principle identified by Sigmon (1979) states that the participants control the service(s) provided. The end of life community forum is designed to be a public forum with participants being able to individualize their learning. The participants are responsible for identifying what resources they require to obtain the information they need. Students are available to help the participant identify needs and to direct them to the correct resources for the information needed to answer their questions.

Service Learning Principle Two: Enabling Participants

Sigmon's (1979) second principle states that service learning enables the participants to serve and be served by their own actions. Participants are encouraged to recognize their own educational needs concerning end of life, to identify goals, and to develop a "map" to assist in acquiring the information required to meet the needs. Students can assist the participants by helping to plan the "map" through the end of life forum. Obtaining information and accessing community resources will allow the participants to obtain their goals.

The multidisciplinary team members reap educational benefits through networking with each other. The networking would provide an opportunity to learn new and innovative accoutrements that would enhance their services.

Service Learning Principle Three: Student Learning

Sigmon's (1979) third principle states that students are learners and retain some control over what is expected to be learned. Students should be given an opportunity to review what they have learned. Students are working with a multidisciplinary team to develop the end of life community forum. They will be acquiring knowledge of the following:

1. Assessing community needs for end of life information
2. Planning a multidisciplinary approach to provide such information
3. Actually accessing the community resources and recruiting them to participate in the forum
4. Hosting the forum
5. Evaluating the effectiveness by participant comments

End of life issues are not always addressed thoroughly in nursing curricula. Students will develop a better understanding of the needs of participants and the community resources available to assist with end of life issues.

This professional conference and community forum provides many opportunities for education, some of which can be service learning based. Repetition of such opportunities can only enhance the community, multidisciplinary teams, and students learning about end of life care.

Reference

Sigmon, R. (1979). Service learning: Three principles. *Synergist*, 8(1), 9–11.

INTEGRATION OF SERVICE LEARNING AND COMMUNITY-BASED NURSING EDUCATION CONCEPTS INTO THE CURRICULUM: THE EXPERIENCE OF RESEARCH COLLEGE OF NURSING

Dr. Nancy Debasio

The nation and its health professionals will be best served when public service is a significant part of the typical path to professional practice. Educational institutions are the key to developing this value. Schools should institute a service-learning requirement for all students, beginning with matriculation and continuing through graduation.
(O'Neil & the Pew Health Professions Commission, 1998)

During the last ten years, there has been a consistent call for change in the education of health professionals. The American Association of Colleges of Nursing (1990) in its landmark report, "A Vision of Nursing Education: The Next Decade," made three recommendations: development of skills in critical thinking and clinical judgement should be the top curricular priority; nurses should be prepared to practice across multiple settings, several of which will be nontraditional; and nursing curricula should increasingly emphasize primary health care, patient education, health promotion, rehabilitation, self-care, and alternative methods of healing.

In its recent curricular revision, Research College of Nursing identified the need to begin a structured implementation of community-based education and the integration of service learning. Each of these concepts is consistent with the missions of the jointly sponsored nursing program. Research College of Nursing, a specialized college of nursing, has engaged in a partnership with

Rockhurst University, a Jesuit institution, to offer the baccalaureate degree. The Research College of Nursing's mission states that "the academic community provides an atmosphere conducive to the development of the individual in scholarship, leadership and service. The college encourages faculty and students to provide leadership and service that fosters community growth." Within the context of the mission, the purposes of the college also serve to denote a commitment to the development of values that support community service. Rockhurst University summarizes its mission in the words "learning, leadership and service," which reflect the belief that a Jesuit education develops men and women for others. Students of Research College of Nursing are members of both educational communities and are able to enjoy the integration of service learning throughout their liberal arts and professional coursework. As freshmen, all students participate in the Finucane service project that is held during freshman orientation. The focus of this project is directed toward meeting the needs of the neighboring communities, including sweeping and general cleanup, gardening, and other such activities. The concept of service learning continues to be reinforced throughout the first semester of the freshman year in the freshman seminar program. It is at this time that the service learning transcript is introduced. The Center for Service Learning coordinates all service learning activities during the educational program. Students develop a portfolio of their experiences that may then be utilized for career placement or for support for other volunteer opportunities such as the Jesuit Volunteer Corps. As will be noted later in the chapter, nursing students complete these forms for service completed in their Professional Practice coursework. During Senior Week, graduating students have the opportunity to participate in the Van Ackeren service project as a culmination of service activities.

As a natural extension of the Research College mission, the faculty identified service as an elected outcome in 1991 as they began preparation for the newly revised accreditation process instituted by the National League for Nursing. Service was defined by the faculty as both curricular and extracurricular. "Curricular service is that service which is provided by students and faculty within the context of the curricular plan and course content. Extra-curricular service is that service in which students and faculty participate beyond the scope of the curriculum." It was essential to indicate that service provided within the context of the curriculum, including activities such as school health screenings, health promotion, and education programs, would otherwise have been unavailable to those served. For example, students in the first sophomore course were responsible for conducting well over 5000 school health assessments in area parochial schools where no school health service was available. As part of their clinical experience, students in the junior and senior years participated in the Rockhurst University Health Fair held each March for all students, staff, faculty, and members of the surrounding community.

In order to develop the concepts of community-based education and service learning, several strategies were identified. Two faculty participated in the Fuld workshop on community-based education in June 1999, which served as a pivotal point in the actual creation of a plan to structure the curriculum around those concepts. One of those faculty assumed the position of chair of the Integration of Nursing Centers Task Force, whose charge it was to design a plan for this integration. During the past academic year, the committee developed the following four basic tenets upon which the plan was built:

1. Community-Based Education (CBE) is a strategy for teaching that works collaboratively with groups of people (including faculty, community members, business leaders, informal leaders, and others) in a way that focuses on assets they bring to solve the problems that they identify.
2. CBE is empowerment education for members of the community.
3. CBE requires ongoing partnerships between education and the community whereby each community becomes a unique context for education.
4. CBE involves educational experiences that generally are associated with community nursing and that encompass a variety of services that emerge from the needs and the capacities of both the community and the educational setting.

The plan was based on several key documents, including the *Essentials for Baccalaureate Nursing Education* (American Association of Colleges of Nursing, 1998); the *Essentials of Baccalaureate Nursing Education for Entry Level Community Health Nursing Practice* developed by the Association of Community Health Nurse Educators (ACHNE, 1990); *Healthy People* 2000, which further confirmed the focus on the need for accessible health care, health promotion, and disease prevention; and the final report of the Pew Commission, in addition, concepts from Rothman (1990) and the Consensus Conference in the Essentials of Public Health Nursing Practice and Education (1985) were utilized to further frame the CBE plan, *Recreating Health Professional Practice for a New Century*. The communities were chosen based on long-standing relationships with grade schools where specific needs were demonstrated within each of these areas and to which the college felt a strong commitment. Thus, the goal of the task force was to incorporate existing centers that are managed by the college and that had a history of providing both clinical as well as service learning experiences.

Blenheim Community Health Center, the Research College of Nursing's faculty-managed health center located in a neighborhood elementary school, and the Rockhurst University Health Center, which is managed by one of the college's nurse practitioners, were identified as the foundational centers for the implementation of this plan. Blenheim Health Center was established in 1996 through support by a Division of Nursing Special Projects grant that facilitated the provision of primary health care services to an underserved minority population. The center serves approximately 800 individuals in the neighborhood and provides physical examinations for day care workers, school sports, camp, and jobs. The school boasts a 100% immunization rate, which is unparalleled in the city school district. In addition, students provide nearly 100 health education programs and screening activities annually to the elementary school students and the community as a whole. Rockhurst University Health Center has been in operation since 1992; it is located on the Rockhurst campus and provides a variety of health care services as well as health education programs for students, staff, and members of the Jesuit community. Both undergraduate and graduate students engage in clinical learning at the site as do family practice residents from a nearby residency program. In addition, two other neighborhoods were identified based on defined needs expressed by the community, experience of the faculty with the site, and relative proximity to the college. A fifth community, which surrounds another faculty-managed community health center, was identified to be used as an additional resource when needed.

The CBE plan is guided by the nursing process, which is reflective of the AACN Essentials of Baccalaureate Education and will be implemented through the team structure. In Professional Practice I students are assigned to one community in which they will remain for all of their community clinical experiences (except in some cases where students may choose to do their service learning in a different site). Team I incorporates course work focusing on skills and technologies, health assessment, pathophysiology, and nutrition (sophomore spring semester) and includes the first Health Management, Professional Practice, and Seminar courses that occur in the fall semester of junior year. The focus of Team I in its professional practice course is on assessment. Team II focuses primarily on analysis, diagnosis, planning, and implementation (delivery of care) through the second two professional practice courses. Team III, which includes Professional Practice IV and the Capstone course, focuses on evaluation and revision. Students will also focus on the roles of designer, manager, and coordinator of care. Team II and III students will assist faculty in the initiation and strengthening of community partnerships. The themes that will be threaded throughout are poverty, multiculturalism, accessibility, health promotion, and disease prevention. Supporting content will be provided in each team's course work to enhance students' understanding of such concepts as the need for community-based education, the neighborhood assessment process, the culture of poverty, the quality indicators of Healthy People 2010, multiculturalism, epidemiology, nursing safety in the community, and systems theory. The task force was also mindful of the need to balance clinical experiences in the acute care environment—as a part of the community learning experience in order to meet the identified needs of hospitals in the greater Kansas City area with the need to prepare graduates to function across multiple settings. Thus, the task force proposed a delineation of actual clinical time that would be devoted to community-based clinical experiences. At this time, the plan is as follows: Team I will provide 67 hours or 30% of total clinical hours to community experiences; Team II will provide 113 hours or 25%; Team III will have a more variable percentage of hours ranging from 11% to 100% depending upon where individual students choose to do their last Professional Practice course and their Capstone course. Students may choose a community site for one or both of those courses. The goal of the CBE plan is to have students engage in community-based clinical learning for a minimum of 22% of their total clinical experience.

In conjunction with the development of the CBE plan, the faculty evaluated the need to more clearly identify and structure service learning experiences. Although they had defined service as an outcome, there was little organization to the manner in which service learning activities occurred. In May 1999 at the Annual Spring Curriculum Workshop, the following proposed definition of service learning was presented:

> Service learning is a teaching learning method which students learn and develop through organized service that: motivates civic and social responsibility; enriches the academic curriculum; meets the needs of the community and is coordinated with an institution of higher learning and with the community; and provides structured time for reflection on the service learning experienced.

This definition was based on "Writing the Community: Concepts and Models for Service Learning" (AAHE, 1999) and the National and Community Service Trust Act of 1993 definition of service learning. It became quite evident that service learning must be integrated within the context of the CBE plan in order to ensure a consistent and meaningful experience for students and for the community. Faculty made the decision that fifteen service learning hours would be required as a component of the first three Professional Practice clinical courses. As noted earlier, students would be given the opportunity to choose their sites or they may choose to remain in the community to which they were assigned in their first Professional Practice course. Faculty shared the belief that structured service learning activities that were required within the context of clinical hours would emphasize their importance. They also believed that articulation of service learning activities would further reinforce an understanding of their social responsibility to others as a critical element of their role as emerging health professionals. Guidelines for service learning are included in the syllabi for Professional Practice I, II, and III; service learning is optional for senior students in Practice IV. However, approximately 25% of the students chose to continue service learning activities. Service learning reflection guidelines encourage students to explore the impact of these experiences on self-understanding and the perceived benefit to their nursing practice. As noted earlier, students who wished to have service learning activities transcripted could do so following completion of the appropriate transcript form and submission to the designated faculty member.

The majority of the service learning activities to date have occurred at Blenheim Elementary School due to the fact that there was a demonstrated need for a myriad of services and a strong relationship with parents, teachers, and staff was already in place. Students designed monthly bulletin boards that emphasized themes such as healthy teeth, safety, and fitness. Students went out in pairs to evening day care parent suppers to distribute information about the services provided at the health center and to poll groups regarding their concerns about health and parenting. Student reports were used to plan for future evening programs that were held by the center nurse practitioners for these parents. Information gathered was also utilized to prepare future health center newsletter articles by service learning students. Several service learning students led by one of the seniors worked with the after school "Visions" program every Tuesday afternoon providing a weekly health presentation selected by the children or the program coordinator. Due to the senior student's leadership in this effort, the health center received an award from the Missouri State Legislature in June of 1999.

Students also learned that service is not always measured in numbers of contacts made or other such quantifiable means. A group of students worked on the presentation of a fitness seminar for parents that was to be held directly after school. Teachers and staff were also invited. Students set up child care, including fitness activities and snacks for the children; prepared health education materials; and were prepared to take blood pressures of staff and parents. One student had prepared the actual fitness presentation. Only one teacher appeared to have her blood pressure taken! Disappointment was momentary; the notion of a needs assessment was placed in its proper context, and much processing occurred about the impact of this experience in terms of understanding the values of the community in relation to determinants of health. The student who had prepared the presentation wrote an article that was then published in the "Health Notes" Newsletter that was distributed to the entire school community.

Lastly, students participated in the organization of the first walk-a-thon to generate support for the health center. Students sought sponsorships from individuals and corporations, recruited walkers, distributed health information on the day of the walk, prepared food, and led the cleanup detail. They often found that their commitment to the health center and its mission was not as widely supported by local vendors. However, at the completion of the walk-a-thon, as children, parents, teachers, college faculty and students gathered, it was clear that each saw the genuine sense of reciprocity between the college, the health center, and the community and the intrinsic value of these relationships to the health of the community as a whole.

The college has also initiated an international service learning experience in conjunction with its partner, Rockhurst University. It was mutually designed by nursing faculty and health project staff in La Labor, Guatemala to meet the needs of the community and to provide a lived experience for students with Guatemalan families. During this one-week period, students gain an understanding of health care delivery in a third world country where extreme poverty prevails and leads to problems of access to health care and lack of education and to issues related to social justice as a whole. Students worked collaboratively with volunteer medical staff as well as indigenous clinic staff to provide immunizations, delousing and deparasiting programs, and vision screenings. Health information was distributed to victims of Hurricane Mitch who were being housed in a primitive resettlement area. Students were stunned by the level of poverty and the lack of basic hygiene, sanitation, and housing and yet were touched by the people's willingness to invite them into their community. Reflections of students following these week-long projects revealed a more clear sense of values and sense of self, an enhanced sensitivity to diversity and differences in communication, a greater awareness of the factors within a community that determine its health, and a more balanced understanding of one's own personal and professional roles. As one student shared, "I came into nursing to change the world; after my Guatemalan experience, I realized that my role as a nurse will be to understand the world better to act on people's behalf." The Guatemalan project will continue to evolve as a service learning experience through feedback from the students, faculty, the project staff, and the community of La Labor. Two students have had the opportunity to participate in each of the annual project weeks. Their insights into the changes that occurred in the community as a result of their first visit were invaluable in the evaluation of the second project week. Their personal commitment to the concept of service learning as an integral component of their professional growth and their civic responsibility has strengthened the college's efforts to engage all nursing students in service learning activities across the curriculum.

Evaluation of service learning activities from faculty, students, and community partners has been for the most part positive. Student comments indicated that often what they received from the community in terms of enhanced communication skills, increased level of critical reflection regarding the impact on their experience on their professional practice, and an overall greater understanding of human existence and potential far outweighed what they had provided. Faculty evaluation of service learning activities indicates that service learning does, in fact, enrich the curriculum as well as the personal and professional growth of the students. They also believe that service learning provides an opportunity for increased student autonomy in areas that are inclusive of both nursing and nonnursing activities. It is important to note that faculty have experienced some challenges in the implementation of service learning activities and the development of a community-based education. There was some resistance to change and a concern for "giving up" clinical time for required service hours when the curriculum was already overloaded. In addition, there were expressed concerns over disciplinary boundaries. Who would be the "community experts" if all faculty were responsible for these community-based service learning activities? The faculty on the Integration of Nursing Centers Task Force recognized and addressed these issues as well as the perceived sense of loss of some sites as they dialoged with their colleagues on each team. The faculty believe that the implementation of the community-based education (CBE) plan will provide the necessary structure for the articulation of service learning activities with community-based concepts and curricular themes. The plan will further support the mission of the college in its efforts to provide an academic atmosphere that will be conducive to the development of all of its students in the areas of leadership, scholarship, and service.

The author would like to acknowledge the work of the following faculty and staff: Dr. Elaine Hardy, Associate Dean; Ms. Michele Haefele, Chair of the Integration of Nursing Centers Task Force; Ms. Diane Darrell; Ms. Karen Cooper; and members of the Integration of Nursing Centers Task Force.

REFERENCES

American Association of Colleges of Nursing. (1990). *A vision of nursing education: The next decade.* Washington, DC: Author.

American Association of Colleges of Nursing. (1998). *Essentials of baccalaureate nursing education.* Washington, DC: Author.

American Association of Higher Education (1999). *Writing the community: Concepts and models for service learning.* Washington, DC: Author.

Association of Community Health Nursing Educators. (1990). *Essentials of baccalaureate nursing education for entry level community health nursing practice.* Washington, DC: Author.

O'Neil, E. H., & the Pew Health Professions Commission. (1998). *Recreating health professional practice for a new century.* San Francisco: Pew Health Professions Commission.

Rothman, N. (1990). Toward description: Public health nursing and community health nursing are different. *Nursing & Health Care, 11,* 481–483.

U.S. Department of Health & Human Services. (1985). Consensus Conference on the Essentials of Public Health Nursing Practice and Education. Washington, DC: Author.

U.S. Department of Health & Human Services, Public Health Service. (1991). *Healthy people 2000: National health promotion and disease prevention objectives.* Washington, DC: Author.

INDEX

Note: Italicized page numbers indicate a figure. The italicized letter *t* following a page number indicates a table.